10 DON'TS ON YOUR DIGITAL DEVICES

THE NON-TECHIE'S SURVIVAL GUIDE TO CYBER SECURITY AND PRIVACY

Daniel G. Bachrach

Eric J. Rzeszut

Apress®

10 Don'ts on Your Digital Devices: The Non-Techie's Survival Guide to Cyber Security and Privacy

ISBN-13 (pbk): 978-1-4842-0368-2

ISBN-13 (electronic): 978-1-4842-0367-5

Managing Director: Welmoed Spahr
Acquisitions Editor: Robert Hutchinson
Developmental Editor: James Markham
Editorial Board: Steve Anglin, Mark Beckner, Ewan Buckingham, Gary Cornell, Louise Corrigan, James DeWolf, Jonathan Gennick, Robert Hutchinson, Michelle Lowman, James Markham, Matthew Moodie, Jeff Olson, Jeffrey Pepper, Douglas Pundick, Ben Renow-Clarke, Dominic Shakeshaft, Gwenan Spearing, Matt Wade, Steve Weiss
Coordinating Editor: Rita Fernando
Copy Editor: Robin Perlow
Compositor: SPi Global
Indexer: SPi Global
Cover Designer: Anna Ishchenko

Distributed to the book trade worldwide by Springer Science+Business Media New York, 233 Spring Street, 6th Floor, New York, NY 10013. Phone 1-800-SPRINGER, fax (201) 348-4505, e-mail orders-ny@springer-sbm.com, or visit www.springeronline.com. Apress Media, LLC is a California LLC and the sole member (owner) is Springer Science + Business Media Finance Inc (SSBM Finance Inc). SSBM Finance Inc is a Delaware corporation.

For information on translations, please e-mail rights@apress.com, or visit www.apress.com.

Apress and friends of ED books may be purchased in bulk for academic, corporate, or promotional use. eBook versions and licenses are also available for most titles. For more information, reference our Special Bulk Sales–eBook Licensing web page at www.apress.com/bulk-sales.

Any source code or other supplementary materials referenced by the author in this text is available to readers at www.apress.com. For detailed information about how to locate your book's source code, go to www.apress.com/source-code/.

Apress Business: The Unbiased Source of Business Information

Apress business books provide essential information and practical advice, each written for practitioners by recognized experts. Busy managers and professionals in all areas of the business world—and at all levels of technical sophistication—look to our books for the actionable ideas and tools they need to solve problems, update and enhance their professional skills, make their work lives easier, and capitalize on opportunity.

Whatever the topic on the business spectrum—entrepreneurship, finance, sales, marketing, management, regulation, information technology, among others—Apress has been praised for providing the objective information and unbiased advice you need to excel in your daily work life. Our authors have no axes to grind; they understand they have one job only—to deliver up-to-date, accurate information simply, concisely, and with deep insight that addresses the real needs of our readers.

It is increasingly hard to find information—whether in the news media, on the Internet, and now all too often in books—that is even-handed and has your best interests at heart. We therefore hope that you enjoy this book, which has been carefully crafted to meet our standards of quality and unbiased coverage.

We are always interested in your feedback or ideas for new titles. Perhaps you'd even like to write a book yourself. Whatever the case, reach out to us at editorial@apress.com and an editor will respond swiftly. Incidentally, at the back of this book, you will find a list of useful related titles. Please visit us at www.apress.com to sign up for newsletters and discounts on future purchases.

The Apress Business Team

This book is dedicated to our respective wives and children: Julie and Sam, Eliana, Jake, Jessica, Caleb, and Lilah Bachrach; and Raya and Sophie Rzeszut. Thank you for all of your support during the writing of this book. We could not have done it without you!

Contents

Contents

Foreword

Men have become the tools of their tools.

—Henry David Thoreau

Henry David Thoreau nailed this observation back in the 1800s, and we can only amplify the meaning of this statement in today's ever-changing digital landscape. The tools we use today, while they are amazing, have the potential to enslave us as a society.

Times, they are a changing, for sure.

I spend a lot of time thinking. My wife calls it spacing out, but I prefer the term "thinking" for right now. I look back a lot; I reflect. I spend a lot of time reflecting about tech stuff and how it's evolved into what it is today. In my 41 short years on this earth have seen some amazing innovations. I've seen the personal computer come into my home. I remember the day my dad brought home a dot matrix printer and the wonderful soothing noise it would make as it shed ink on that perforated paper. I remember typing lines of basic code into a computer console to display "HELLO" on a black and white gigantic CRT monitor. This "stuff" that's been created is nothing shy of amazing, and it's the little things in technology that really wow me. With the hard drive, CD-ROMs, wireless mice, smartphones that have more processing power than the first computers at NASA, it is truly an amazing time to be alive. It's even more amazing how all of these gadgets and gizmos are interconnected and talking to each other. Enter the Internet.

The Internet has been an amazing contribution to society. It has enabled us to connect in ways that we never knew possible. It has allowed for the rapid dissemination of news and information. It has both brought us closer as people and pushed us further apart on an interpersonal level. The Internet has connected everything. Cars are now connected via Wi-Fi hotspots, your new refrigerator has the capability to sync with your Wi-Fi, you can control your home alarm system or even your air-conditioning by simply pushing a few buttons on your smartphone. With all of this connectivity in the home, in the workplace, in your car, in your doctor's office, in your Facebook and Twitter feed, there are data. Rich, unfiltered, personal, revealing data. These data can be used for good, but, let's be real, these data can also be used for evil. As amazing as the Internet is, it's bred a whole new breed of crook: cyber criminals. They are lurking everywhere. From foreign countries to your local coffee shop, cyber crooks are stealing data and profiting from those data at an alarming rate.

Data equal gold. With a few keystrokes or the accidental installation of malware on your computer, you can give hackers access to your life. Your dreams, your vices, your finances, your secrets—hackers can get it all, and once they have it, your whole world can be corrupted. There are millions of e-mails sent each second that are designed to trick you into giving up your personal information. There are weak firewalls at your doctor's office that a hacker can breach to steal your personal medical information and sell it on the various black markets found in the shadiest, darkest recesses of the Internet. There are exploits in the security certificates that you think are secure when you are purchasing your whatnots from your favorite online retailer. There are weak, hackable Wi-Fi connections at your favorite big-box retailer that a hacker, sitting in his Ford Fairmont in the parking lot, can access and then pull down thousands of credit card numbers through the air in minutes.

Again, data are gold, so how do you protect yours? How do you keep your personal credit from being destroyed or your medical records sold to Sally in Baltimore who uses your medical history and credit to get some enhancements done? How do you keep snooping social media platforms from listening in on your verbal conversations through your smartphone or search engines from taking all of your search data and building a profile on you?

For some folks, technology is downright scary and intimidating, and rightly so. I remember the first time my grandmother logged in to Facebook and the look of panic on her face as she clicked her first unsolicited pop-up ad. Grandma had become a master of the copper landline phone system, but she was now facing a whole new world. A world not connected by copper wires, but a world of millions of interconnected devices, all talking to each other. I remember my dad, as he would call me for countless tech trivia questions about installing and uninstalling Windows on his laptop. Technology can be your friend, but it can also be your worst enemy. Dan and Eric have crafted a sound, educational, and user-friendly road map to help keep your data safe and your tech devices protected. *10 Don'ts* was written with a passion—a passion to inform and educate, a passion to help keep you safe in an ever-changing digital world. If you're intimidated by your tech devices or are eternally worried about keeping your data safe and secure, this book is for you.

Remember, while the Internet has many downsides and a veritable host of creepers, it is also an amazing, rich, and powerful tool to help your mind grow, to help you connect with long-lost friends, to inspire you, to help you create amazing content, and, of course, to add countless photos of your cat. Use it wisely, maybe back off of the cat photos, but enjoy it safely and with common sense.

Tom Jelneck

President, On Target Web Solutions

Tom Jelneck lives in Orlando, Florida, with his beautiful wife, two daughters, and a Siberian husky. Jelneck owns and operates two businesses in Orlando. On Target Web Solutions (OnTargetWebSolutions.com) is a digital marketing agency, and The Contentinators (TheContentinators.com) is a digital content creation company that supplies high-quality copywriting and visual graphics for digital marketing campaigns.

Jelneck is also the tech expert for WOFL-Fox 35, Orlando and has appeared in over 200 segments discussing all things tech and security. Jelneck has also appeared on CCTV, WESH-NBC Channel 2, News13 Orlando, and has been interviewed by USA Today regarding e-mail security. A sought-after speaker, Jelneck has presented at numerous tech and marketing conferences. Jelneck can be found on Twitter @ontarget.

About the Authors

Daniel G. Bachrach, PhD, is a Morrow Faculty Excellence Fellow and professor of Management at the Culverhouse College of Commerce at the University of Alabama. He has published extensively on employee and team performance drivers, transactive memory systems, and organizational citizenship behavior. He also is coauthor of the books *Transformative Selling: Becoming a Resource Manager and a Knowledge Broker and Management 13e* and is co-editor of *The Handbook of Behavioral Operations Management*: Social and Psychological Dynamics in Production and Service Settings.

Eric J. Rzeszut is an information technology and security professional (CISSP) with two decades of experience in the industry. Eric is the Help Desk manager at the University of Virginia's McIntire School of Commerce. Previously, he was an IT manager at the University of Alabama at Birmingham (UAB) and a founding member of the UAB Enterprise Information Security Council. He regularly makes information security presentations and consults to a variety of academic, nonprofit, and corporate groups.

Acknowledgments

Dan Bachrach would like to gratefully acknowledge his senior colleague at the University of Alabama's Culverhouse College, Professor Ron Dulek, *New York Times* best-selling author, for his generously given advice, guidance, and willingness to offer honest critical feedback when it would have been so much easier to not give it.

Eric Rzeszut gratefully acknowledges the support of the information technology staff at the University of Alabama at Birmingham (UAB); the faculty and staff of UAB's Department of Cell, Developmental, and Integrative Biology; and particularly that department's chair, Dr. Tika Benveniste, for her many years of support.

In addition, many thanks are offered to the faculty and staff of the McIntire School of Commerce at the University of Virginia as well as the university's Information Security, Policy, and Records Office (ISPRO) for their support, advice, and guidance.

Introduction

We hear it every day, on television, on the radio, at the grocery store, and at the movies—that our world is getting smaller. We can be anywhere in the world within a day, by jumping on a plane, and with Skype, Google Hangouts, or Apple's FaceTime we can talk face to face to almost anyone in the world with broadband in the time it takes to turn on the computer or other mobile device. We can get any book, magazine, journal article, movie, television show, or newspaper going back more than a hundred years, and we have essentially limitless, immediate access to all of the publicly available recorded information from the beginning of modern record keeping.

Almost any and all information that we could possibly ever need or want is available to us at the speed of electricity, and our lives are infinitely better for it in uncountable ways. Research and practice in medicine, science, health, art, music, language, travel, and a myriad other domains has increased exponentially as a direct consequence of the immediate availability of information that we take for granted in the 21st century.

While we all take advantage of this magnificently available connectivity in different ways, the overwhelming sociological trend across race, age, gender, generational, and other demographic categories is that as a society we're becoming more connected to one another and not less. In fact, virtual connectivity has become so ubiquitous a concept in our culture today that variation in our levels of virtual connection to one another has come to be recognized as an element of human personality.

For example, recent survey research reported by Broadcom Corporation on more than 2,500 American adults identified seven distinct "connectivity personality types." Nearly half of those participating in the Broadcom survey were identified as either "Always On," "Live Wires," or "Social Skimmers," all of whom maintain very high levels of Internet presence. In contrast, only 2 percent of those surveyed fell into the "Never Minders" category, with essentially no level of social media or Internet interaction whatsoever. The overwhelming majority of us are, apparently, connected at least sometimes to the overwhelming majority of us online.[1] As a society, we're being collectively redefined at least in part by our patterns of virtual interconnection.

---

[1]BusinessNewsDaily, Chad Brooks, "What's Your Technology Personality Type?" www.businessnewsdaily.com/3557-technology-personality-types.html, December 10, 2012.

Living in the interconnected world we've created and defined carries risks with it, and sometimes potentially very steep costs and difficult-to-recover-from consequences as well. We essentially now live in a globally connected virtual neighborhood and the immediacy and connectedness we enjoy on the one hand directly implies that the neighborhood isn't always safe—not in the conventional sense. Not everyone living in the globally connected community that defines most of our lives in a broad range of fundamental ways is thinking about it in an adaptive, collective-goods focused way.

There are thieves who with criminal self-interest and purposeful guile would do you harm and steal your last dollar and good name if given the opportunity to do so. Unfortunately, on the other side of the wireless network connecting you to libraries and shopping and books and movies and friends and all of the data you use every day are criminals who are actively trying to steal your passwords, your personal information, your identity, and your money. This vulnerability is in large part an inherent consequence of the nature of the architecture that supports the Internet itself. It was not designed to be a fortress or to allow for the selective retention of safe spaces or neutral zones. For example, as Tony Townsend, information security analyst at the University of Virginia, argues: The Internet uses an antiquated design. Originally, there wasn't any thought of keeping people out—the Internet was designed to be open, to share data, to let people in. All of today's methods to prevent break-ins and keep the bad guys out have been added after the fact.

This isn't a trivial concern. Enormous dollars and resources are at stake. Time spent trying to regain lost opportunities, damaged reputations, and heartache are real costs paid by the millions of victims of virtual crime, when intellectual property, identity, and livelihood are lost or threatened through the theft of proprietary data. The illegal acquisition and use of your personal information—social security number, credit card accounts, bank accounts, checking accounts, and passwords can fundamentally change your life in terrible, unrecoverable ways.

Criminals are waiting for you to make a mistake so they can get your password(s) when you inadvertently give them access. Criminals can get all of your passwords and access to all of your sensitive accounts when you install unwanted, hidden software (malware) on your computer, tablet, telephone, or other mobile device(s) that we increasingly take for granted as members of the information age. Criminals also attack from the other side of the virtual landscape, critically compromising the information technology, infrastructure, and systems of large corporations to steal their customers' critical financial data and access their personal records.

The financially devastating and widely publicized attack against mega-retailer Target in late 2013 leveraged both internal and external avenues of vulnerability. A phishing attack (discussed in Chapter 1) allowed the thieves to access the credentials of a contractor working for Target. A poorly designed security infrastructure then allowed the credentials of that contractor, an HVAC company, to be used by the thieves to access the financial data of millions of customers, which they had no legal right to access.

It's not only criminals who are interested in getting their hands on your data. It is essential to not lose sight of the fact that larger, somewhat less ill-intentioned bodies also want access to your identity—at least parts of it. Your online identity is being constantly impinged upon, probed, evaluated, examined and recorded. This is being done not by criminals actively seeking to steal from you, but by bodies toward which we (at least some of us) ascribe relatively more benign intentions. Corporations and the government maintain an active, focused interest in you, your online persona, and what you do while you spend time connected to the Internet.

While corporations (hopefully!) aren't seeking to steal your password(s), they do want to know your spending habits—in detail, what other sites you are actively interested in, how much time you spend browsing, what clicks you make, and what keeps your eyes on one site vs. another. They are interested in your demographics and family information and your exercise, travel, recreational, interpersonal, and consumption patterns. They want to know all about you. They use the information they collect about you to directly micro-target their advertising specifically to you and more effectively set the hook for their own products and services—rather than those of competing firms also seeking your business.

The government also is very interested in you and what you are doing online. It wants to listen to your phone calls, to see what you have on your hard drive, and to monitor what you send over the Internet and Wi-Fi networks. It is interested in your e-mail, how you spend your money, where you travel, and who your friends are. Some of the surveillance that the government maintains is legal. Some is not. Many surveillance practices fall into a gray area, and their legality is being hotly debated, even today.

Although many of us would say that we have nothing to hide, some of the documents recently released by former US government contractor Edward Snowden—now living in Russia—are quite disturbing. For example, Snowden claimed in a July 2014 interview that National Security Agency (NSA) analysts routinely pass around the nude photos of innocent civilians intercepted by NSA operatives over the Internet. Access to these private, nude photos was considered a "perk" of the position according to Snowden and not seen in any way as a violation of civil liberties or an otherwise taken-for-granted right to privacy.[2] What remains is that, today, big brother really is watching and is

---

[2]Ars Technica, Cyrus Farivar, "Snowden: NSA Employees Routinely Pass Around Intercepted Nude Photos," http://arstechnica.com/tech-policy/2014/07/snowden-nsa-employees-routinely-pass-around-intercepted-nude-photos/, July 14, 2014.

paying very close attention to you and to what you're doing when you spend time online.

One of the emergent realities of the connectedness that defines our personal and professional lives today is that increasingly our "valuables," broadly defined, are not stored in physical locations or guarded by a lock and key. The most crucial strategic assets that banks hold are no longer stored in a giant safe in the basement with a combination lock and an armed security guard.

They are stored digitally in cloud space, protected by advanced mathematical fences and "impenetrable" dynamic algorithms. All "neighborhoods" are connected in the digital or online world. An axiom of the information age that we live in is that the openness that makes our immense progress possible also invites unwanted and unavoidable virtual proximity to real dangers. These dangers take the form of real criminals as well as overbearing intrusive authority and commercial interests that impinge on our treasure and personal liberties.

We're experiencing an ongoing, slow-moving shift of perception that also contributes to the dangers that users face. Today, although credit cards, PayPal, virtual money, check cards and other "clean" currency modalities (including the emergent Bitcoin, an entirely virtual and nationless currency) have become universal and ubiquitous, as a society we still retain an attachment (perhaps psychological, perhaps emotional) to thousands-of-years-old, archival, value transmission tools like the dirty coins and paper bills we carry around with us in our pockets.

As a society, we're still not comfortable with the redefinition of what is valuable today, or where this "value" resides. As an example, most of us would never take a wallet out of our pocket or purse and leave it on a conference room table or on someone's desk at the office while we run down the hall for 10 minutes. This would be crazy because there are valuables in that wallet—$89 in cash, a Visa, and a punch card to Yogurt Mountain that is one punch away from a freebie! Yet, in the modern American workplace an exact corollary of this unthinkable decision happens all of the time with smartphones, tablets, and laptops. In many ways the theft of one of these powerful data storage and delivery devices is likely to be significantly more financially consequential to the owner than the theft of his or her wallet.

In fact, more often than not the data stored on a digital device are significantly more valuable—and the costs of recovery significantly higher—than the device itself in which the data are stored. If an end user's laptop is stolen at the airport, the cost of the physical device (maybe $1,000 today) is likely covered by insurance, either personal or corporate, depending on who owns the device. Even if it's not covered by insurance, replacement is getting increasingly affordable. But the data stored on the device may take scores or hundreds of labor hours to re-create—or may even be completely unrecoverable. The theft also might lead to vulnerabilities in an organization's communications infrastructure or networks, potentially exposing the personal and financial data of millions of customers, and costing millions and millions of dollars in recovery, damaged reputation, public relations rehabilitation, lost future business, and sunk resources.

The somewhat over-used term "hack," while still part of our popular vernacular, has recently been supplemented by a new, more accurate descriptor: the "Advanced Persistent Threat," or APT. While the term "hack" brings to mind a single action taken at a specific time, APTs are, as the name suggests, advanced and persistent. They're always out there. The attackers may take weeks or months to develop their assault, tracking the organization's behavior and IT infrastructure, probing for weaknesses, and developing the most effective way to attack.

Modern users can't simply secure their devices and watch their behavior at only certain times, or in certain places. APTs are constant and adaptable, and the vigilance of those potentially vulnerable to these modern attacks must be constant and adaptable as well (see Figure 1).

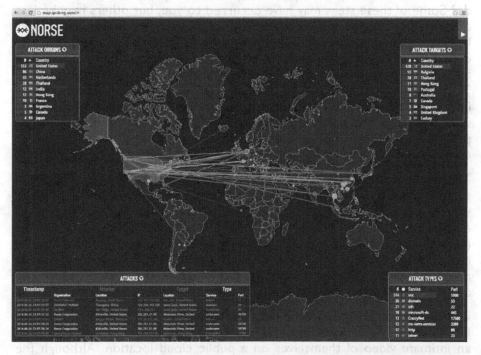

Figure 1. This live map, produced by the Norse Corporation, shows a real-time view of the origins and targets of digital attackers worldwide. (map.ipviking.com, used with permission)

The Internet that we all use, and increasingly take for granted as a functioning reality of our professional and personal lives, is in actuality an interconnected global network—which is simultaneously both a really wonderful place and a really dangerous place. Because it provides us with the immediate access to data that we rely on in so many fundamental ways, it also puts our own personal data at risk. So, given that we can't pick and do not get to choose who comes into and out of our virtual neighborhood, what can we do? Although this is a frightening scenario, and the threat is real, there are ways to protect yourself against these evolving, ever-present dangers. In this book, we address approaches that users can adopt to minimize modern virtual threats.

The passwords that you use to limit access to your intellectual property and to your sensitive online accounts can slow criminals down. Choose them wisely, use them, protect them, and change them if they've been compromised. Follow the advice of experts. Communications from your corporate IT department and official e-mails from merchants with whom you trade should not be spammed or ignored. When they advise you to create a stronger password or to change your password, listen!

Lock your digital "property" up by protecting it with passwords that limit access to it. How do you keep your important property safe? What can you do? Some of these steps may have occurred to you, but others may be less obvious. Don't use an unsafe computer or public network to do private tasks like online banking. Obvious? Not necessarily. A lot of us like to work at the coffee shop, or get a few minutes of work done at the airport. Don't use ancient (here, read more than a couple of years old), unsupported devices. The technology in newer devices offers more sophisticated protection against intrusions that weren't in existence when previous generations of machines were designed and produced. Don't use outdated operating systems or programs. As these tools erode relative to the context in which they're embedded, thieves can take advantage of emerging security cracks.

The capabilities associated with, and our use of, the Internet are changing in such fundamental ways that many of us today don't really even understand where we store the important documents and data that we use. As a consequence, concerns and even genuine fear about online data storage (i.e., "in the cloud") have begun to pervade popular culture. This kind of reaction is common when new tools and approaches are widely and quickly adopted while a majority of the people who use the tool or adopt the approach don't really understand its strengths or limitations.

In the summer of 2014, Sony Pictures released the film Sex Tape, in which Jason Segel and Cameron Diaz play a married couple who accidentally store an intimate video of themselves on a public cloud location. Although the technical details portrayed in the film aren't 100 percent accurate, it plays on the average computer user's ignorance (and fear) of the cloud. As Segel's character exclaims in rage, "No one understands the cloud. It's an f-ing mystery!" Yet, despite our uncertainties about what the cloud is, and the implications of its use, there are safe (perhaps *safer* is a more appropriate term here) ways to use cloud storage and cloud application providers, which we discuss in detail in the following chapters.

Keep your computer up-to-date and use antivirus software. Even if you run a firewall, if you let your protection get outdated, newer threats will be more likely to escape the protective net it offers. Don't try to use an old, outdated operating system (e.g., Windows XP) or an ancient phone or tablet. Here, "ancient" is broadly defined as any mobile device older than two or three years. The protections available through modern operating systems are essential to keep criminals from encroaching on your data today, but this has not always been so.

Don't give strangers access to your private financial data. Be very careful whom you allow to access your accounts and files. When non-family members have access to your home, your wireless network, or your devices, take precautions to protect yourself against unauthorized access to your data. We focus on some of these precautions in the chapters of this book.

Take prudent, informed steps to protect your most sensitive data from the scrutiny of corporations and government entities that operate with their own agenda in focus. Don't give commercial organizations access to or allow the government to access your Internet search history or activities online. What can you do to avoid this kind of snooping? Keep reading.

When traveling—for business or pleasure—take extra precautions to keep your data safe. Airports and hotels are very popular target sites for the physical theft of digital devices. Open Wi-Fi networks in airports, convention centers, and coffee shops can easily be hacked. Don't transmit sensitive data over any wireless network that doesn't require a password. Avoid using hotel business center computers whenever it's possible to do so—who knows if the last person to use that computer was a hacker! Turn off the Bluetooth on your phone if you don't need it, and don't let a stranger at the airport use your phone or computer. What can you do to increase the physical security of your devices at home, at work, and in transit? We discuss these issues in detail in Chapter 10.

Don't go into dangerous sites on the Internet. Don't try to get music, movies, or software for free on sites where these kinds of giveaways are advertised. More often than not—way more often than not—there's no free lunch when it comes to software or other applications. The much greater likelihood is that by visiting a tempting site that advertises freebies you will only make yourself vulnerable to infection and heartache.

If it seems like it's too good to be true—just like the drop-the-fat-pills that don't work and the knives that allegedly never get dull—it probably is. More than likely, the supposedly "free" stuff is going to come packaged with a virus or other malware that will dig right into your computer and open the door for criminals to access your personal data. Develop a healthy sense of paranoia and skepticism when it comes to your data.

Why do criminals want your virtual property? There is big money—*big* money in identity theft. This is among the fastest growing crimes in terms of damages, a $375 billion-a-year crime that affects one in 25 Americans every year. Of course, not all of this identity theft is limited to crimes occurring over the Internet or in digital contexts.

People do still steal credit card statements from mailboxes, but the per capita incidence of digital crimes is on the rise, and it is increasing every year. Unwanted software, or what is referred to in technical circles as malware, is sometimes just written to cause havoc and is essentially an act of cyber vandalism, but far more frequently these programs are intended to generate profits for the criminals who write and deploy them. And they do—enormous profits.

So, how do criminals get your property anyway? There is never going to be a 100 percent secure fix or an absolutely airtight solution to the problem of unwanted intrusion or theft of your property. If a criminal is determined enough, he'll eventually break in one way or another. In reality you take security precautions so that the potential risks associated with theft of your property outweigh the potential rewards, so that the thief chooses another potential target.

It's not ultimately the integrity of a security system that serves as a deterrent to thieves trying to steal your property, but the potential costs of doing so that keep your property from being stolen. This is the same with all of the digital property that you'd like to keep safe. If you don't make it easy for criminals to get access to your private data, the cyber thieves who'd otherwise steal from you will move on to easier targets who've not protected themselves adequately. We'll show you how to keep your data safe.

The simplest way for thieves to get access to your property is by you making it easy for them. Your digital property is more likely to be stolen if you make mistakes like these:

- Your password is the word "password" or the digits "123" or your first name, etc.

- You leave your computer, phone, or tablet unattended at a coffee shop, or open and available when other people are in your home.

- You click links in an e-mail indiscriminately, without stopping to think (or find out) if they are legitimate.

- You store data indiscriminately in "the cloud" without considering the ramifications of doing so and/or the policies of your workplace.

- You don't change your password even after you think someone else might have learned it.

- You ignore warnings from corporate or consumer IT professionals concerning password strength, reuse, and retirement.

- You don't have a pass-code on your smartphone, even though you keep a list of account numbers or passwords on it.

- You connect to open, public Wi-Fi networks and transmit sensitive data over these unsecured channels.

- You visit "bad neighborhoods" on the Web, entering your e-mail address, password, and other private information in an effort to get free software, music, or movies.

- You use an ancient computer without updating your operating system or software applications.

More often than not people don't maintain even the most remedial precautions protecting their virtual property. You'd be surprised at the kinds of mistakes that otherwise well-informed, intelligent, professionals make when it comes to protecting their data from theft. Thieves will still try to trick you into letting them in even if you've got security in place. Unfortunately, end users fall for these tricks all the time. Thieves use the Trojan horse approach as it pertains to your digital property. Criminals may call on the phone and try to get your password by pretending to be someone authorized to have access to your information, someone you trust, like a network administrator or a company representative. Maybe they'll send you a "phishing" e-mail, trying to get you to click on a link that looks legitimate, and then provide your password or other personal information to a third party who will sell it or use it themselves. Maybe they have a free, open wireless network in a public place. Of course free public Wi-Fi is convenient, but are thieves stealing your data while you're using their air? Maybe they'll have a free app for your smartphone or tablet that makes wonderful claims—but is it stealing your data instead? We discuss these issues in depth in the pages that follow.

Successful criminals are clever, and they're getting more so all the time. When one avenue for theft or fraud is blocked, they'll find others. Just as nature builds a better mouse to avoid mousetraps, the approaches that criminals employ are also constantly evolving in the face of responses to the threat posed by their criminal activities.

Phishers and other data scammers will prey on human nature, using a psychological strategy called "social engineering." They'll attempt to learn more and more about their targets before making contact, increasing their odds of hooking an unsuspecting phish. They'll take advantage of human nature and our inclination to be kind, pretending to need assistance or adopting other approaches to gain sympathy and encourage potential victims to make themselves vulnerable to attack. They might also impersonate a person of authority, demanding access or the entering of a password, preying on our tendency to follow the rules and to respect authority. They'll often hint or explicitly state that their request bears on a critical, time-sensitive issue, giving the targeted victim no time to think. They'll use every trick in the book to get you to do what they ask.

In the end, it is critical to be very suspicious of people seeking access your data. Obviously, not everyone on the Internet is a criminal interested in stealing from you. But, the criminals are out there and it's best to be prepared. In this book, we develop a straightforward, linear approach for doing just that. We hope you find what follows to be useful to you as an informed, connected, active citizen of the 21st century.

Don't Get Phished

Stay Out of the Net

Joe is a midlevel procurement manager with 14 years of experience at the multinational company Worldwide, Inc. His section is a large one, and much of the procedural updating that regularly comes through official channels is disseminated virtually—by text, the corporate instant messaging application, or e-mail. Joe rarely sees his immediate supervisor during the course of an average day and is accustomed to getting—and following—electronically delivered policy and housekeeping directives. Joe's communications with administrators from other sections in his division also typically come through company e-mail. From time to time updates to the company's IT systems require him to change his existing passwords or create new ones, so he is not uneasy when he receives a routine e-mail from his company's IT group directing him to update his system password (see Figure 1-1).

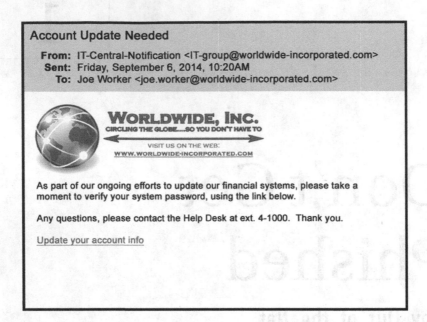

Figure 1-1. Sample e-mail asking for password confirmation and featuring two hyperlinks: the company logo and the "Update your account info" line

The e-mail is fairly well-written and looks kosher. It employs quasi-proper English grammar, incorporates the company logo in the usual way, and is signed with the correct phone extension for the IT help desk. The message contains a hyperlink to the company's web site and another for Joe to confirm his existing password and set a new one.

Joe nearly clicks the second link but hesitates when he remembers that upcoming system password changes are announced at the weekly section meeting and that he can't recall such an announcement having been made at the last one. He hovers his cursor over the hyperlink and is alarmed to see that it would take him not to his company's domain (Figure 1-2) but to a malicious domain (Figure 1-3).

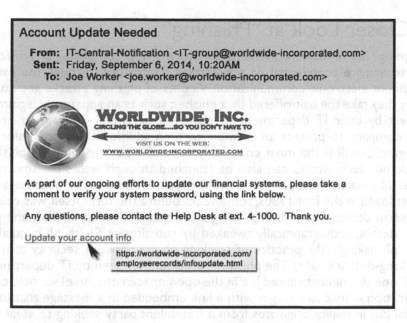

Figure 1-2. Joe hovers his cursor over the account update hyperlink, expecting it to give his company's domain name, as shown

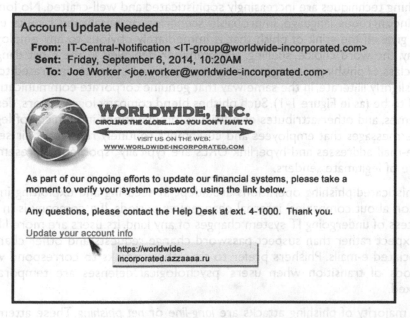

Figure 1-3. Joe instead sees that the hyperlink would take him to a malicious domain

A Closer Look at "Phishing"

"Phishing" is a virtual attack that uses a more or less compelling or attractive lure to acquire confidential or proprietary information through the use of fraudulent electronic communication. Victims of phishing attacks get caught when they take the bait offered by a phisher, such as an apparently legitimate request by their IT department to change a password or by their credit card company to protect an account with an additional personal information gate. E-mail is the most commonly used approach to launch a phishing attack, but such attacks can also be launched through web sites, text messages, IM (instant messaging), and mobile apps. Phishing techniques began to be deployed in the late 1980s, some years before the term itself was coined. The term derives from "fishing" for gullible users' login credentials and personal details, orthographically tweaked by substituting *f* with *ph* by analogy with "phreaking" (the practice of cracking phone network security to make free long-distance calls). The phish most commonly seen by IT departments is the one that almost snared Joe in the opening scenario. An electronic communication is sent to a target with a link embedded in a message that looks official but in reality originates from a fraudulent party seeking to steal personal information in order to gain malicious access or to resell to a criminal cyber organization.

Phishing techniques are increasingly sophisticated and well-crafted. No longer are incongruous language, improbable scenarios, or misaligned layouts used that give off the stink of phish that is immediately obvious to any employee. Today, the word choice, spelling, and grammar deployed in the most dangerous class of phishing messages are correct or, even better, are calibrated to be just slightly illiterate, in the same way that genuine corporate communications tend to be (as in Figure 1-1). Such phishes blend company logos, colors, design schemes, and other attributes of official communications in mimicry of legitimate messages that employees and customers routinely receive. Their sending e-mail addresses and hyperlink URLs are typically "spoofed" to resemble those of legitimate senders.

Sophisticated phishing operations are adept at securing and exploiting information about companies' internal changeover periods. If a company is in the process of undergoing IT system changes of any kind, its users are more likely to expect rather than suspect password change requests and other change-associated e-mails. Phishers prefer to time their attacks to correspond with periods of transition when users' psychological defenses are temporarily relaxed.

The majority of phishing attacks are *long-line* or *net phishing*. These attempts don't have a specific target. Their goal is to snare as many victims as possible following a volume or economies-of-scale approach and leveraging a broad, randomized targeting scheme. Contrasted with this kind of broadcast phishing is *spearphishing*, which is carefully and lethally aimed at a specific individual, company, school, or other organization. These kinds of attacks are much more dangerous than conventional untargeted phishing scams.

"Target"-ed Phishing

A targeted spearphishing attack may be deployed to go after someone specific, such as Joe, because the attackers are aware that he has a system account with access to sensitive company information. A general, untargeted phishing attack may go out to literally tens or hundreds of thousands of mailboxes or phones. If even a few of the targets click on the malicious link, the attack is a success. Spearphishing attacks, on the other hand, target a defined group of users or even only one high-value user within an organization.

One of the troubling characteristics of contemporary phishing is the range and versatility of tactics attackers use to lure or lull victims into providing valuable information. For example, in phone-keypad phishing, users are told to dial a number that a caller says belongs to the end user's bank or credit-card company but that is in reality owned by phishers. End users enter their account number, social security number, PIN code, or other private information via the telephone keypad, which is then captured and sold or used by the phishers.

Phishers use *cross-site scripting* (CSS or XSS) to compromise legitimate sites with pop-up windows or browser tabs that redirect users to fraudulent web sites. CSS attacks are more prevalent on computers and systems with unpatched and/or outdated operating systems (for more, see Chapter 8).

Neutralizing phishing is not a trivial issue. What's at stake? Money. Most phishers are in it purely for financial gain. EMC's 2013 annual report estimated that $5.9 billion was lost worldwide to nearly 450,000 phishing attacks. This same report identified a hacking tool called Jigsaw that allows malicious actors to gain specific and detailed employee information for use in spearfishing attacks. With access to your bank account information and password, phishers can easily transfer funds away from your accounts or divert a paycheck or other direct deposit away from your account to accounts that they control.

Phishing also increases personal and organizational exposure to malware. For example, in November 2013 malware called Zeus was spread via attachments to phishing e-mails that claimed to contain important system and security updates. Once installed on a PC, Zeus detects banking, credit card, and other financial information entered by the end user and reports those credentials back to a compromised server. Reputable antivirus manufacturers such as Sophos and Norton issued statements immediately reminding users that no legitimate software manufacturer would ever send out security updates by e-mail attachment. Within a short time all the commonly used anti-malware programs, such as Microsoft Security Essentials and Sophos Antivirus, added specific protections against the Zeus malware to their security definitions. The users most at risk from malware are those who neglect to use continually updated anti-malware software.

But, it's important to recognize that criminal phishers don't limit themselves to attacks on little phish. Sometimes, they target and land the big phish as well—sometimes the whale. The well-publicized attack on Target Corporation that evolved over the course of several weeks during November and December of 2013 was likely instigated through a phishing attack on a Target contractor. In this massive security breach, more than 10 million Target customers' credit card numbers were stolen. A heating, air-conditioning, and refrigeration firm headquartered in Pittsburgh, Pennsylvania, Fazio Mechanical, reported a phishing attack on its systems. This attack was responsible for the delivery of a password-stealing piece of malware called "Citadel" that ultimately was the mechanism used to breach and compromise Target's systems.

The malware attack at Fazio Mechanical is believed to have begun two months before the Target Corporation was, well, targeted. In addition to suffering a massively expensive public relations black eye, Target also directly shoulders some of the technical/operational responsibility for the loss of customers' credit card information. Target failed to properly segregate its information systems infrastructure broadly—and its customer credit card databases specifically—from virtual corridors connecting directly to outside contractors. An HVAC contractor simply shouldn't have access to Target Corporation's customer credit card data! But this breach, which turned out to have been one of the largest in U.S. history, was most likely catalyzed directly by an employee at Fazio who was tricked into clicking a link that just shouldn't have been clicked. Big storms start with small breezes…

Other Forms

Criminal phishing attacks aren't limited to an approach through e-mail. For example, SMS phishing or "smishing" is a similar kind of attack, but one that is executed through the use of text messaging to potential victims' mobile phones. Users receive a text message that their bank, credit card company, or other financial institution (credit union, student-loan company, etc.) needs them to reconfirm some aspect of their on-file personal information for records updating. This request could include anything from a user's social security number to his mother's maiden name to the specifics of the checking account used to pay monthly invoices. Absolutely no topic is off-limits.

On a similar tack, voice phishing is called "vishing." With vishing, attackers use automated voice systems with which they can impersonate a bank or other robocaller. We're all familiar with these calls today, getting them regularly from financial institutions or other sources, reminding us of appointments, of an upcoming event, or of changes in policy. Vishers can also often "spoof" the caller ID on the targeted victim's phone, making it seem as though the call actually originates from a legitimate organization—even one from the user's own contact list.

Criminals today are extremely flexible in the approaches they adopt. They take advantage of a wide range of common vehicles to camouflage their activities. Some of these are fairly new, so most users today haven't developed the kind of healthy caution they might otherwise have when interacting with a more familiar potential delivery mechanism for malware. With QRishing, criminals play on our familiarity with—and excitement about—the now ubiquitous QR bar codes used in advertisements, on cereal boxes, and on a host of other products we see every day. Unfortunately, this particular convenience is as susceptible to parasitical encroachment as other modern vehicles. A QR code may say, for example, "Scan this to win a prize," while in reality it installs a piece of malware directly onto your phone or computer.

And, of course, social networks are not immune from these kinds of attacks. Phishing scams are extremely common on Facebook and Twitter. "Click here to win free airline tickets." "Click this for free games." Phishers will use embedded links in communications masquerading as content coming from your friends, your work, your place of worship—any source you might trust—all with the goal of enticing you to click.

As we discuss in depth in Chapter 9, these are all types of "social engineering" approaches that attackers use to prey on our human nature to achieve their goals. They'll use the threat of lost or found money ("You'll be charged $5/day unless you click here" or "You can win $1,000!"), authority ("Your supervisor requests that you enter your password here"), or immediacy ("There's an emergency and we need your information immediately!"). Nothing is too devious or out of bounds, no message too sensitive, no concern too sacred.

Adopting a slightly different bearing, "USB-ishing" is an approach that attackers use to lure potential victims into plugging an unknown USB flash drive into their computer. Attackers will leave attractive, high-capacity drives in conference rooms, rest rooms, hotel lobbies, or other public places where they are likely to be found by unsuspecting phish. When a user connects the flash drive to a computer, the USB drive then automatically installs a Trojan, a key logger, or other malware onto the user's machine—most often without the user knowing it's been delivered.

This particular point of vulnerability may also have a broader, underlying structural problem. In July of 2014, security researchers Karsten Nohl and Jakob Lell demonstrated that USB drives are inherently unsafe by design. At the Black Hat security conference, these researchers demonstrated that malware can actually be hidden in the firmware of a USB device—the very software that controls the device itself. By concealing malware in the physical artifact in this way, it is undetectable by modern anti-malware software. Even more troubling here, the malware stored in firmware in this way is not removed when the drive is erased and or reformatted.[1] Because USB flash drives are so incredibly useful, and because most of us use them every day for even our most sensitive data, the results from this report are chilling. Any USB drive that has ever been out of our direct control is vulnerable. What's becoming increasingly clear is that the very fine line between security and usability continues to get thinner and thinner every day!

What Should You Do?

To avoid the potentially grave personal and financial costs of falling prey to phishing, like Joe, develop habits of reflexive suspicion and jealously guard your personal data. Unattractive traits in face-to-face situations are virtues online and can help to keep you safe (or at least safer).

Your suspicions should be raised if you receive an unsolicited e-mail or IM, click on a web site, or receive a phone call that asks for any of the following types of highly sensitive information:

- Your password
- Your bank account information
- Your employee ID or social security number
- Other private data

You should never provide any of these sensitive data via e-mail. E-mail is inherently insecure—there is no such thing as a private e-mail. This basic operational fact of virtual exchanges in the 21st century means that no legitimate organizational representative would ever ask you to provide this kind of information via e-mail.

Over the phone or on a web site, caution is no less essential. If you have any doubts about the legitimacy of a caller or a web site, make contact using a familiar, established, and assuredly valid channel, such as the phone number or the web site printed on the back of your credit card. Look closely at any e mails that claim to come from your bank, credit card company, mortgage company, or employer. Be suspicious. Are the colors in the logo a tad off or is the overall look not quite right? Are there any oddities of expression, slovenly spellings, or grammatical hiccups?

---

[1]Wired, Andy Greenburg, "Why the Security of USB Is Fundamentally Broken," www.wired.com/2014/07/usb-security/, July 31, 2014.

If you are ever asked in an e-mail to click a link, study it with gimlet eyes. Hover your mouse pointer over the link to see where it is going to take you before you click. Phishers rely on end users to be too hurried or distracted to notice clues that would emerge on closer inspection.

Look at the end of the web address—not the beginning or the middle—to see if it's truly the site that it purports to be. If you click the link and go to the page, evaluate the page using the same criteria as you would when evaluating a suspicious e-mail. Look critically at the logo, colors, spelling, grammar, and vocabulary for any signals that something is awry. If it is, go no further. You could be putting your sensitive personal and professional data at risk—and putting your company's servers and all of their systems in jeopardy as well.

Unless you're perfectly confident an e-mail or web site is legitimate, don't enter any data. If you're working for a firm with an IT department, get in contact with your section IT supervisor. If you are on your own, seek out and ask a reputable source about the e-mail or the web site. If it's your credit card company, bank, or other financial institution, call the phone number on the back of your card or on your billing statement to determine whether the contact is legitimate or not.

If you're at all suspicious about an e-mail, do not reply to it. If you reply to a phishing e-mail with questions seeing clarification, the phishers will just lie to you and tell you whatever they think you want to hear. You represent no more than a criminal mark to them. E-mail is simply not a secure method of communication for any kind of critical information. E-mails can be hacked or intentionally or accidentally forwarded to others; anyone with an official purpose is wary of these inherent limitations.

It is important to forward suspicious e-mail to your IT supervisor, if you work for a firm with an IT group. The IT consultants can confirm whether or not the e-mail you received is a phishing e-mail. They can also often block or otherwise prevent that particular sender from reaching any of the computers or systems at your company again. If you realize only after clicking a link and entering personal data that it's suspect, you should immediately take the following steps.

First, change all passwords and other identifiers that you provided to the suspect site. This will stop or retard phishers' efforts to make direct use of your data. If you entered work-related data, notify your immediate supervisor and the IT area supervisor at once. It is essential that the right sequence of remedial protections be initiated to try to limit the spread of damage. If you entered personal credentials or financial data in reference to your bank account or credit card company, notify those companies immediately. When cleaning up a phishy mess, it is especially important to use channels that are above suspicion, such as calling the phone number on the back of your card or on your statement or visiting your local bank branch in person. The crucial and inviolable rule is to never to send passwords or other private data via e-mail.

Although it's out of the hands of the "average user," e-mail providers also are doing what they can to intercept phishing attacks before they reach users' in-boxes. In August of 2014, Google announced that it would be implementing new anti-phishing mechanisms for its enormously popular e-mail service, Gmail. Google will now restrict the use of Unicode characters—characters in non-Latin alphabets, or alternates to Latin characters—when used in certain combinations designed to trick people. For example, replacing the letter *a* in "OnlineBank.com" with a Greek lower-case alpha wouldn't be noticeable to most end users (see Figure 1-4). But with the proliferation of international web domains that allow non-Latin characters, the user could unknowingly be taken to an entirely different web site.[2]

OnlineBank.com
OnlineBank.com

Figure 1-4. Most users would never notice (or understand the significance of) the difference in these two URLs. The top link is typed in standard Latin characters; the second link replaces the lowercase *a* with a Greek lowercase alpha

Be cautious and take steps to protect yourself from non-e-mail forms of phishing. Be suspicious of unsolicited text messages and phone calls. Be careful when scanning any QR codes. Use common sense when looking at links on your social networks, links that purport to be from your "friends." If something seems too good to be true, it probably is! When in doubt, contact your friend via a known-to-be-good method (e-mail, phone, text) and ask if she sent you a particular link. Don't use USB flash drives that you find somewhere or that are handed out, and be cautious when lending USB drives to someone else (and then getting them back). On all of your social network sites, always watch your links!

---

[2]Google Official Enterprise Blog, Mark Risher, "Protecting Gmail in a Global World," http://googleenterprise.blogspot.com/2014/08/protecting-gmail-in-global-world.html, August 12, 2014.

Additional Reading

For more reading on how to keep away from phishers and their bait, see the following links, and visit our web site at www.10donts.com/phished.

- Microsoft Safety & Security Center, "How to Recognize Phishing Email Messages, Links, or Phone Calls," with examples of these various types: www.microsoft.com/security/online-privacy/phishing-symptoms.aspx

- Norton Security, "Spear Phishing: Scam, Not Sport," featuring a discussion of how spearphishers attempt to gain information on their targets: http://us.norton.com/spear-phishing-scam-not-sport/article

- OnGuardOnline (produced by the US Department of Justice), "Phishing Scams," which includes methods for reporting phishing attackers: www.onguardonline.gov/phishing

- PayPal, "Can You Spot Phishing?", a quiz that tests the reader's knowledge of common and uncommon phishing attack vectors: www.paypal.com/webapps/mpp/security/antiphishing-canyouspotphishing

- Sophos.com, "Simple Steps to Avoid Being Phished," www.sophos.com/en-us/security-news-trends/bestpractices/phishing.aspx

- Stay Safe Online (powered by the National Cyber Security Alliance), "Spam and Phishing," with some good general advice: www.staysafeonline.org/stay-safe-online/keep-a-clean-machine/spam-and-phishing

Don't Give Up Your Passwords

Keep the Keys Safe

Jackie, a newly hired HR database administrator (DBA) at a major state university, has several years' professional experience working with big data. In her first week Jackie is "on-boarded" into the position. She is immediately granted full access to a large number of university systems and databases, which have disparate password and access requirements. Because of an absence of coherence across departments and university subunits (which is typical of large organizations), Jackie has to learn several new logon procedures for these assets. Some of the more sensitive systems at the university depend on "two-factor" authentication, requiring Jackie to use a physical identity (sometimes called an authentication or cryptographic) token in combination with a password.

In order to keep all of these passwords and protocols straight as she learns the ins and outs of her new position, Jackie writes them down under the desk blotter at her workstation. Jackie's physical work space is an open cubicle. Because cubicles keep no secrets, one of her coworkers notices this practice. She warns Jackie that, in addition to being extremely dangerous practice, writing down passwords in an unsecured location is actually grounds for termination from the university. She shows Jackie how to use a password app on her smartphone, protected with a master password. This app can be used to secure the passwords and logon procedures required for Jackie's job. If the phone is secured with a personal identification number (PIN), and the app is secured with a master password, this password management scheme is approved by her university.

Where Did Passwords Come From?

The first computer passwords were likely used in the mid-1960s on the mainframe system at the Massachusetts Institute of Technology (MIT).[1] In the earliest days of personal computing, protective gates like passwords were essentially irrelevant because of the small numbers of sophisticated users actually involved in this emerging technology. Early broadly publicly available computers purchased by civilian end users, such as the Apple II series, the first Macintosh, and the IBM PC and PCjr didn't even incorporate a logon password option. End users simply turned on the computer and the machine automatically loaded the desktop, no questions asked. Everything on the machine was immediately available to anyone who could push the "on" button.

Microsoft Windows versions 95, 98, and Me allowed for the adoption of a security password, but didn't actually require users to enter the password to log on to the machine! These operating systems simply allowed users to press Esc at the login window, which then granted immediate access to files, software, and data (see Figure 2-1)—literally at the push of a button. Functionally, passwords became a much more critical operational finger-in-the-dike with the emergence of early online services (AOL, CompuServe) and the increased, broad-scale usage of e-mail and other on-line services through the Internet.

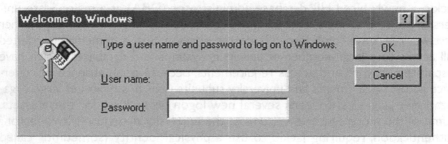

Figure 2-1. The logon box for Microsoft Windows 95, 98, and Me allowed the user to simply press Cancel (or the Esc key) at this dialog, and full access to the operating system was granted, without a password

Passwords became increasingly necessary to protect end users' identity as Internet communications became more common. Passwords are, in part, intended to ensure the integrity of online identity. Early password protection offered some assurance that if an incoming e-mail was identified as having come from "Jackie" that the recipient could have confidence it was coming from Jackie. As the nature of the ways we use our computers has

---

[1]Wired, Robert McMillan, "The World's First Computer Password? It Was Useless Too," www.wired.com/wiredenterprise/2012/01/computer-password/, January 27, 2012.

continued to evolve, and the transmission and storage of more—and more critical—information is increasingly taken for granted, passwords have become more important to us.

Their importance is matched by our dependence on the data and information they protect. As technology and computing tools have become integral to modern work performance and broad-spectrum social activity in society, passwords have become much more essential, and as a consequence they've also become more vulnerable to attack. As a fact of modern information exchange *we use e-mail for everything*. If the password to an e-mail account is compromised, a criminal can potentially gain access to checking accounts, credit card information, and other vital personal and customer-related data. Because of an inflated sense of personal privacy, the ease of use inherent in the interface, and a general complacency about personal security, e-mail has become a favored point of entry for hackers to essentially limitless access to private information.

Password Threats and New Solutions

Hackers have a wide range of tools and points of leverage with which to gain illicit access to e-mail accounts. However, there are several *most common* attacks criminals use to crack security precautions. The "brute force attack" leverages a dedicated computer, or series of integrated computers, to apply a mathematical algorithm that essentially guesses and tries all possible passwords within a system. This approach tends to work very well against shorter passwords but is much too time-consuming for longer passwords. This is one of the reasons that IT administrators are increasingly requiring 12-character (or longer) codes. The entry hurdle increases as password complexity and system security are heightened.

In contrast with the brute force attack, which requires substantial computing power (and time), with a "dictionary attack" an algorithm is employed to guess all of the most common passwords that can be found in a dictionary. This approach is very efficient. Because all possible combinations of letters aren't being tried—only dictionary words—it can be executed much more quickly. The English language is estimated to encompass just over a million words. Deployed correctly, a "modern" computer can enter 1 million words into a security portal's password checker in less than 24 hours. *Daisy, rainforest,* and *butterfly* (all common passwords) don't stand a chance against a concerted attack.

There are substantial financial and reputational costs associated with the loss of critical customer data (i.e., social security numbers, credit card numbers, checking account information, home addresses, etc.) In early 2014, the online auction giant eBay suffered an alarming data breach when criminals stole the login credentials of several employees. This enabled access to eBay's corporate databases where the thieves misappropriated the personal data (login names, passwords, addresses, and phone numbers) of as many as 200 million eBay customers.

Alternatives to the "Simple" Password: Biometrics and Two-Factor Authentication

Some cutting-edge systems are beginning to incorporate biometrics (most frequently fingerprint readers, but at higher levels of security in corporate or government contexts retinal scanners also are seeing increased use) as an alternative to conventional passwords. In the retail sector, for example, the Apple iPhone, as of September 2013's "5S" model, leverages an integrated fingerprint reader that can actually be used in lieu of a pass-code. Phone manufacturers Samsung and HTC also have added this feature to their newest devices. Consistent with the broadening trend toward more sophisticated (or more convenient?) entry hurdles, many laptops now also incorporate fingerprint scanners as a security gate. These come with various packages of features, depending on the model and manufacturer, attached in conjunction with the scanner itself.

Credential-based attacks (i.e., a stolen password) have recently been waged against Adobe, Twitter, Kickstarter, and Apple. The "Data Breach Investigation Report" released by Verizon in April 2014 found that two of three data breaches in 2013 involved criminals using compromised or misused credentials. In light of these recent attacks (which depended on the compromise of a simple username/password), more and more organizations have begun to institute what is called "two-factor authentication" or TFA. TFA increases the information hurdle necessary for access to secured internal systems, requiring users to provide two of three (or more) system "factors."

Users have to *know* something, typically a password or a pass-code, which represents an entry hurdle similar to that of a conventional password portal. Users also must *have* something. This could be a token of some kind, or a mobile app that provides a randomly assigned code at login, or a text message that includes login-specific information. Alternately, some TFAs incorporate something that end users *are*. This could be something physical or biometric and might be captured through fingerprint or retinal scan. In the future, this biometric factor might also even encompass DNA matching.

Because the TFA requires that two of these three factors be available for system access, the odds of random or unauthorized entry, or entry through a concerted illicit attack, decrease dramatically. If a criminal captures a password, via phishing attack or other means, the system is compromised for only one of these system elements. Thus, the system remains protected because access within TFA is precluded without two factors in place at login. If eBay had had two-factor authentication in place in February 2014, a stolen password alone would not have allowed attackers to access millions of users' personal and financial data. However, as with "Jackie" at the beginning of the chapter, writing down passwords in an obvious location entirely negates one of the components of two-factor authentication! Two-factor authentication can function effectively only as a supplement to—not as a replacement for—a strong password policy.

Google introduced a retail-focused, *optional*, two-factor authentication system in 2012. Each time users who request this additional security protocol attempt to log in to Gmail (or any Google service) with their standard password, Google's servers send them a random code via text message, voice message, or the Google app. If the random code isn't entered correctly, system access is denied. Users also have the option of telling Google, essentially, "Don't make me enter a code again when I log in from *this* device," i.e., the user's home or work computer. The "stand-down" option offers the convenience of logging on with fewer security steps from more frequently accessed computers while still protecting users against criminals who acquire their passwords and try to log on from their own (i.e., the criminal's) computer.

Here, readers are likely to recognize that secondary backup security procedures can be somewhat…inconvenient. When different devices are used to check e-mail (for example, during travel or commuting), substantial time can be consumed serially surpassing secondary backup security protocols. This highlights a basic modern operational truth of the open-systems framework into which our devices and our data are integrated. Security and convenience operate in a constant balance. As systems become more secure, they also become more cumbersome. As systems become more convenient, they become more vulnerable. This is a reality.

Bigger Can Be Better…

In light of the inherent give and take in the security-convenience trade-off, most IT experts and professionals recommend that end users think in terms of what are being called "passphrases" rather than "passwords." Longer passwords are mathematically much harder to crack due to the exponentially increasing number of potential combinations of password elements (see Table 2-1).

Table 2-1. The total number of possible permutations increases exponentially with password length

# of characters	Equation	Total Possible Combinations
4	83^4	47,458,321
6	83^6	326,940,373,369
8	83^8	2,252,292,232,139,040
12	83^12	106,890,007,738,661,000,000,000
16	83^16	5,072,820,298,953,860,000,000,000,000,000
20	83^20	240,747,534,123,068,000,000,000,000,000,000,000,000

■ **Note**   This table assumes the use of the 83 possible characters on a standard English-language keyboard.

For example, "*IoncevisitedSt.Louis,Missouri*" is a much stronger password than a simple "*missouri123.*" These kinds of security phrases are harder for criminals to guess, or automated programs to crack, yet are still relatively easy for end users to remember. They also offer a coherent mnemonic for remembering longer key strings that would be exceptionally difficult if the string were composed of randomly chosen characters.

Mix It Up

Whenever possible, different passwords should be used for different sites, particularly sites that store credit card or other financial data. "Work" passwords should be kept distinct from "personal" / social media / photo-sharing / online shopping passwords to segregate spheres of vulnerability.

When hackers steal credentials from a particular web site, these data often are sold to another thief. The buyer may try the stolen credentials on other sites (unrelated to the original), because many people use the same username/ password for most (or all!) of their online activities. When most users hear about a breach at eBay, they will change their eBay password. But what if they use those same credentials and log-on key for Amazon, Google, Zappos, etc? Do they change all of those logins? Unfortunately, most probably don't.

In 2012 Best Buy customers reported unauthorized use of their online accounts to purchase Best Buy gift cards and other merchandise. These users had their credit card information stored on BestBuy.com, but there had been no indication that the retail giant's own servers had been compromised.

Hackers were using credentials stolen from other sites, correctly assuming that many users had the same credentials for their BestBuy.com account.

We believe a secondary party gleaned user information and passwords from other online sites and then they're tapping into us and other retailers to see if people are using their same password across multiple sites.

—Susan Busch, Best Buy's senior PR director

Although end users are typically bombarded by frantic-seeming system administrators with requests for disciplined password protocol adherence, ongoing discussion within the IT security community has left open the question of what is the most effective enforcement approach for password expiration and reuse. It is debatable whether it is a good idea to force users to change passwords on a regular basis, or to prevent them from reusing their last several passwords (which many users would prefer to do).

On the one hand, advocates argue that forcing frequent password changes limits the potential damage that a criminal can inflict once in possession of a user's password. Restricting users' ability to reuse old passwords also prevents criminals from using these recycled passwords to gain access to key accounts and data (or personal financial information). On the other hand, overly restrictive expiration/reuse policies increase the probability that users will forget their password.

Forgotten passwords can lead to productivity losses, as users are forced to go through a password reset process each time the password is forgotten (more information on this issue follows below). This approach also can more easily lead to security breaches, as users who can't remember their passwords are more likely to write them down or store them in other insecure places (like the underside of a desk blotter…!).

Security consultant Bruce Schneier offers a discussion of this situation on his virtual security blog focused on the issue of password policy.[2] Schneier makes the excellent point (unlikely to be found in most corporate or other on-boarding materials), that it's always a good idea to change e-mail, social media, banking, etc. passwords when a romantic relationship ends. Romantic partners often know each other's passwords. This substantially increases the potential collateral damage of failed love. Criminals aren't the only parties interested in your data, and a jilted lover has just the right (or wrong…) motivation to make a difficult-to-clean-up virtual mess of your on-line accounts.

---

[2]Schneier on Security, Bruce Schneier, "Changing Passwords," www.schneier.com/blog/archives/2010/11/changing_passwo.html, November 22, 2010.

Protecting Passwords

When users forget their password(s), as they invariably will, the password reset procedure also is a point of potential system vulnerability. The reset procedure has to be secure but is subject to the same kinds of security limitations as other data transmission processes. How is a new password provided to users? If the password is sent via e-mail, this procedure opens up a host of questions revolving around issues of e-mail vulnerability. Is the e-mail address verified and secure? What gates are up to protect the e-mail against unofficial or illicit appropriation?

What about if the password is sent via phone or text? What kinds of proof of identity are users required to provide within this transaction? Is the new password provided in person? Is the user required to provide some kind of identification? What role does the in-person inconvenience factor play within this approach? There is an inherent trade-off between password transmission security and convenience in this process that limits the range of options that administrators (and users) are likely to accept on a regular basis. If the new password is provided in person, is it handed to each user on a physical slip of paper? If it is, what's to prevent users, like "Jackie," from simply keeping that slip of paper in plain sight on their desk or, even worse, up on their dry-erase board?

Likewise, if a physical identity token is provided, what steps are taken to ensure users' identity? How does the administrator verify that the person is who he says he is? What about remote users who need an identity token but are unable to conveniently make an in-person visit? Is this feasible? What if it's the e-mail account of a sales rep in another state, or the account is attached to an office in another country? What steps are taken to ensure that the token is being given to a genuine user rather than an enterprising thief with counterfeit credentials involved in advanced persistent threat (APT) reconnaissance and infiltration? Although a techno-thrilleresque prospect, it is not at all a far-fetched scenario today. As we discuss in Chapter 9, brazen on-site impersonation of legitimate company personnel and physical plant penetration are becoming more and more common today.

Is it sent through the mail? This can lead to a great deal of lost productivity as individual users wait for their physical token to arrive. It can be extremely difficult balancing security and productivity needs. As a point of definition, these considerations are often at odds. Individual users will inevitably be inconvenienced by stiffened security protocols.

But, individual users within a larger organization don't operate in a vacuum. Their decisions and actions directly affect that collective. Here, the needs of the many may outweigh the needs of the few. Individual users' productivity can be hampered by heightened security protocols, but one user's security failure has the potential to impact substantially the productivity of the entire organization. If servers go down, a core network is compromised, or clients' personal and financial data are lost, collective productivity can be catastrophically—even fatally—damaged, with eBay being a recent graphic example.

It's important for users to remain cognizant of security threats like these. Although typical users don't administer (or even have access to) frequently used servers, it is essential to pay attention to instructions or warnings disseminated by administrators. As a case in point, in April 2014 a vulnerability called "Heartbleed" garnered wide media attention. Heartbleed is an exploitable weakness in the OpenSSL software used on an estimated two-thirds of the world's public web servers.

This was an entirely "back-end" issue from the "front end," the typical user's interface point, there was nothing users could do to protect themselves from passwords being stolen. The vulnerability had to be resolved from the back end (system administrators). Yet, when the vulnerability was repaired, users were instructed to change their passwords as previous passwords could have been stolen. In the wake of Heartbleed, many organizations and popular consumer sites like Tumblr, Reddit, and Pinterest strongly recommended that users change their passwords immediately.

Twenty-first century end users have to be sophisticated enough to recognize this type of legitimate password advice and to differentiate it from the faux requests / phishing attacks discussed in Chapter 1. In the case of Heartbleed, the probability that any particular user's password on a specific site was compromised was extremely low. But in aggregate, a site like Reddit, which has nearly 3 million regular users, almost certainly had some compromised accounts.

What Should You Do?

Data security and use of password protection simply cannot be an issue that users only casually flirt with. Once it was popularly recognized that vulnerability to sexually transmitted diseases had potentially lethal consequences, condom use was no longer seen as an inconvenience or a choice—it came to be viewed as a requisite ticket to ride. It is critical to adopt an almost life-and-death appreciation of the use of virtual protection today.

Systematically consider your various passwords and very carefully contemplate how you use them. Choose different passwords for each of the services that you use. Or, in light of inherently limited cognitive space and mental resources, choose as many passwords as you can reasonably remember. Avoid the inclination to use a dictionary word of any kind. A pet's name, or any other overly simplistic password can be easily guessed at or harvested through an illicit systematic virtual hunt. Adopt passphrases rather than passwords because they are more difficult to crack. If you can't remember them all, adopt a 21st-century approach and consider taking advantage of a biometric system or leveraging password-management software, as suggested to Jackie at the beginning of the chapter (see Figures 2-2 and 2-3), rather than writing them down somewhere where they can easily be found by others.

Figure 2-2. When using a password manager application such as KeePass, the first step is to set a strong master password, ideally one that the user will never forget. Many applications will give a visual indicator as to the strength of the selected master password.

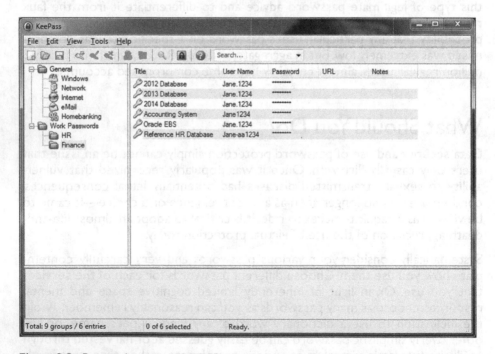

Figure 2-3. Password managers like KeePass can store various passwords for the user, separated into categories. Noteworthy is that these applications can often choose a random password for the user; the user needs to recall only the self-selected master password. (Screenshots from KeePass used under the terms of the software's General Public License [GPL])

It also is critical to recognize that your mobile device is exceptionally vulnerable both virtually and physically. Add a PIN or password to all of your mobile devices. If you think or even suspect that a computer or mobile device of yours has been compromised, immediately change all of the passwords that were used on that computer. (We discuss mobile security specifics in greater detail in Chapter 7 and physical security threats in Chapter 10).

Additional Reading

For more on how to be smart with your passwords, see the following links and visit our web site at www.10donts.com/passwords:

- Google's "Secure Your Passwords" page, with general advice on password intelligence: www.google.com/goodtoknow/online-safety/passwords/

- Microsoft, "Tips for Creating Strong Passwords and Passphrases," with particular focus on the passphrase option: http://windows.microsoft.com/en-us/windows7/tips-for-creating-strong-passwords-and-passphrases

- CNet, "Two-Factor Authentication: What You Need to Know," a good overview of the practice: www.cnet.com/news/two-factor-authentication-what-you-needto-know-faq/

- InformationWeek, "7 Tips to Toughen Passwords": www.darkreading.com/risk-management/7-tipsto-toughen-passwords/d/d-id/1104754

- Lifehacker, "Here's Everywhere You Should Be Using Two-Factor Authentication Right Now," with advice on the best places to leverage this approach: http://lifehacker.com/5938565/heres-everywhere-you-shouldenable-two-factor-authentication-right-now

- PC Magazine, "The Best Password Managers," with reviews of multiple password management systems: www.pcmag.com/article2/0,2817,2407168,00.asp

- Schneier on Security, "Choosing Secure Passwords," advice from well-known security analyst Bruce Schneier on methods of password selection: www.schneier.com/blog/archives/2014/03/choosing_secure_1.html

- Yahoo!, "Should You Use a Password Manager," by Tom's Guide/Elizabeth Palermo, listing some pros and cons of this approach: http://news.yahoo.com/password-manager-144610473.html

Don't Get Lost in "The Cloud"

Stay Grounded

Mike, a formerly self-employed graphic designer, was recently hired on full-time as a marketing associate at Worldwide, Inc. While he was working as a freelancer, Mike made regular, liberal use of cloud-based services like Dropbox and Adobe's Creative Cloud. "Cloud" storage services, which house users' files on servers maintained in the provider's physical plant(s), allowed Mike to access all of his data using multiple devices, from almost any physical location.

Access to these services was essential for sharing designs with clients, collaborating on projects with other designers, and allowing him to work from home, the road, or wherever he happened to be. Mike frequently used the "public" folders in these cloud services to simultaneously share projects and files with multiple stakeholders (see Figure 3-1). In contrast with this open-form approach, his new employer maintains a contract with a specific cloud provider, Microsoft OneDrive. Worldwide requires that all company data stored in the cloud be on OneDrive.

Figure 3-1. Most cloud storage services include (by default) a number of subfolders. One or more of these folders may be publicly accessible to the world at large. Users should take care when storing files in the public folder, and ensure that private/proprietary data are not stored there.

However, because Mike only recently signed on at Worldwide, he is still used to the storage patterns he adopted as a freelancer. He keeps software and work files in his personal cloud accounts. Because he uses some of those data in his new position, he continues using Dropbox and Creative Cloud when it's convenient. He also uses these services when outside contractors (e.g., an offset printer) prefer to use a service other than OneDrive. A couple of months after Mike joined Worldwide, it emerges that some of the company's proprietary data has been obtained by a competitor. Worldwide's investigative team immediately launches a full audit of current data storage and sharing systems to locate the source of the breach. Mike's use of non-approved cloud providers and public storage (available to anyone!) is one of many employee violations uncovered during this audit.

What Is "The Cloud"?

Although the term has become part of the current vernacular and ubiquitous in conversations on issues of data storage, access, and retrieval, there is a lot of misunderstanding and misinformation surrounding cloud computing. Many users put faith in the cloud, and make a host of operational assumptions about the way it functions, but most don't have well-developed answers to the questions "What is 'cloud computing'?" or "What does it actually mean to store data in the 'cloud'?" Given increasing online vulnerability, and a constantly changing cyber landscape, not knowing the answers to these questions can lead to uninformed decisions with extremely serious consequences.

The "cloud," which has become a quasi-technical term, actually refers to a system of networked, physically separated, interconnected computers. The computer (or other equipment) can be in a different physical location from the user, but the size of the network space created by these connections is defined by virtual—and not physical—dimensionality. Users storing data on Google Drive, Microsoft OneDrive, or Apple's iCloud store their data in network spaces defined by virtual connections between computers hundreds or thousands of miles from their physical point of contact with this space.

Practically, cloud computing for average "retail" users wasn't feasible until high-speed Internet connectivity became relatively inexpensive and conveniently available in homes and businesses. Before the data "pipe" could be widened to coincide seamlessly with modern computing requirements, there was no market for the cloud. No one wanted a service that required 20–30 minutes to open a file!

Once affordable retail connection speeds became sufficient, cloud computing gained momentum. Amazon is credited with starting the first major cloud service with the 2006 launch of Amazon Web Services. This allowed external customers, which were primarily small businesses, to purchase storage and application space on Amazon's servers. Several major technology companies have since begun to offer cloud services. These second-generation providers have primarily focused on individual users.

Among these later entrants is Apple, whose service started as MobileMe in 2008, became iCloud in 2012, and added iCloud Drive in 2014. Microsoft launched Windows Live Folders in 2007, which is now known as OneDrive. Google launched Google Docs in 2007, with limited cloud storage, transitioning to Google Drive in 2012. Adobe launched Creative Cloud in 2011. Several relatively new, smaller providers have quickly found success in this growing market as well, including Box, which launched in 2005; Dropbox, which launched in 2008; and CloudMe, which launched in 2011. These providers use a range of business models to sustain their market offerings.

For example, Google uses Drive as a way to tie users into what is broadly known as the "Google Ecosystem." Use of one system in this suite tends to encourage the use of other Google products. Google derives value from this approach because it facilitates a more fluid gathering of customer data, which in turn increases the effectiveness of customer-focused advertisements. Box and Dropbox (among others) offer their basic services for free, with the objective of enticing customers to upgrade their account status to a more advanced fee-based version of the service.

Cloud Controversy and Risks

Propelled by increasing privacy and fair-use sensitivity, the cloud market has seen recent content-domain controversy. In 2012 the photo-sharing cloud service Instagram, now a subsidiary of Facebook, made headlines. Instagram revised its terms of service with ongoing users so that it could use their photos in advertisements at the company's own discretion, with no compensation to end users. After a flurry of bad press in a wide range of trade journals and general media outlets, Instagram reversed its stance and omitted the change-of-service terms.

Instagram did this, even though it had no legal obligation to do so. Instagram had every legal right to change the terms of service with users of its *free* product! When users upload photos, or any other data—be they sensitive client data or employee social security numbers—to a cloud-based service, an explicit agreement has been made to the terms of that service. It is critical to investigate those terms thoroughly before putting your data into the system, to ensure that the host service isn't going to use your data in ways with which you would disagree—or in a manner that could put the privacy of your clients' data at risk.

In light of changing work patterns, and increasing market sensitivities, many corporations, government agencies, and educational institutions have begun to formalize relationships with specific cloud providers. Organizations are realizing that their employees can use these tools to increase collaboration and productivity. If employees are going to use these cooperative tools, the sponsoring organization should follow best practices to avoid unwanted front-page attention.

Formalizing an Informal Relationship

Private consumers use cloud services in a wide variety of ad hoc ways, which is only to be expected in light of both the relative novelty of the service itself and users' far-ranging data storage and access requirements. Public organizations or other large collectives that incorporate the cloud as an element of their official business processes should, however, explicitly formalize all aspects of their relationship with the cloud provider. It is essential to define costs, allotments, and service-level agreements. If you are a manager, director, or supervisor, or occupy another senior-level position in your organization, educate your employees! If they're allowed to use only the sanctioned cloud provider, for example, enforce this directive through well-articulated human resources (HR) or information technology (IT) policies. The way the organization wants the cloud to be used by employees must be clearly indicated in rules bearing on this approach. It is also critical to inform employees about what sorts of data can or can't be stored in the cloud.

For example, the University of Virginia has a partnership with Box, allowing all faculty, students, and staff to have up to 50GB of storage space at no cost to end users. The university defines what kinds of data are allowed to be stored in Box and what types are prohibited. The university also provides formal guidance and written policy on how to share files via Box with non-university personnel. With the goal of limiting collateral damage, the university also strongly discourages faculty and staff from storing university data with any other cloud storage provider. This policy benefits the University of Virginia by standardizing the cloud provider used. It also benefits faculty, students, and staff because they have a substantial volume of storage space available to them free of charge.

However, because it is an "official" collaboration, the university also has to provide technical support for faculty, students, and staff using the service (which is actually another benefit for university personnel). Organizations without an official cloud provider or set of controlling policies may find employees using a variety of cloud services, with no consistency. As with the "bring your own device" (BYOD) trend, the term "bring your own cloud" (BYOC) has been coined to describe employees doing just that. As we saw with our graphic designer "Mike" at the beginning of the chapter, it is critical that even companies with "official" cloud arrangements be aware that their employees may be using "unofficial" or unauthorized cloud providers, and take steps to intercede before a data breach.

Data Breaches

For all the hype surrounding the cloud, there is nothing sacred or pristine about a cloud storage approach to safeguarding your data. These data aren't being kept in an impenetrable vault. The data you store in the cloud are only as safe as systems-in-place make them. Data stored by a cloud service—even a paid service—can be stolen. Numerous recent examples have gotten publicity in the computing press over the last several years.

In 2010, a Microsoft small-business cloud service inadvertently exposed customers' address books to public download. Although the issue was reportedly resolved shortly after being discovered, "illegitimate" downloads of customers' data were detected. *PCWorld* reported that these losses were incurred as a consequence of what a director of communications for the compromised site referred to as "a configuration issue."[1]

---

[1]PCWorld, Andrea Udo de Haes, "Microsoft BPOS Cloud Server Hit with Data Breach," www.pcworld.com/article/214591/Microsoft_BPOS_cloud_service_hit_with_data_breach.html, December 22, 2010.

In 2013, a university-based teaching hospital in Oregon found that physicians and staff in both its Division of Plastic and Reconstructive Surgery and Department of Urology and Kidney Transplant Services were storing patient data, including names, social security numbers, ages, diagnoses and addresses, on Google Drive. Although this practice violated both hospital policy and the 1996 Health Insurance Portability and Accountability Act (HIPAA), the physicians and staff were storing sensitive data on Google Drive to make it easier to share information about patients. The HIPAA-protected data of more than 3,000 patients were exposed to theft. Such incidents are not without precedent at this hospital: mHealthNews reported that in 2009, the personal health information of roughly 1,000 patients was stolen from an employee's unencrypted laptop, and in 2012 the personal health information of 14,000 patients was stolen from an employee's unencrypted thumb drive.[2]

Perhaps most alarmingly in light of the intense focus the topic has received in the media, in 2013 Adobe's cloud services were hacked...again. In what is likely the largest security breach that Adobe has experienced to date, hackers were able to break into Adobe's servers and steal customer names, IDs, passwords, encrypted credit and debit card numbers, expiration dates and other core customer-specific information. This attack exposed nearly 3 million customers to the loss of their most sensitive financial data. *Talkin' Cloud* reported that the actual extent of the damage to customers using the cloud service may never be fully determined.[3] These breaches are occurring not merely with off-brand providers with small security budgets and less-than-current market knowledge. These substantial, costly, high-profile breaches are occurring at top-tier technology firms, with well-established brands and world-class reputations...in the firms' primary domain of expertise.

Not Just for Storage Anymore

Cloud computing has its origins in data storage, but it has evolved to include *applications* as well as data. More and more, software is being offered as a service rather than as a product. For example, Adobe's Creative Cloud bundles graphics, design, and web applications into various suites. In a departure from the conventional retail approach, these products are only sold digitally. Users cannot purchase Adobe Creative Cloud in retail packaging for a one-time fee. It is available only through subscription. Microsoft's Office365 product operates in a similar way with the Office productivity suite.

---

[2] mHealthNews, Erin McCann, "Latest Hospital Data Breach Involves Cloud Services," www.mhealthnews.com/news/latest-hospital-data-breach-involves-cloud-services, July 29, 2013.

[3] Talkin' Cloud, Chris Talbot, "Adobe Data Breach: Will Skeptical Cloud Users Exit?" http://talkincloud.com/saas-software-service/adobe-data-breach-will-skeptical-cloud-users-exit, October 4, 2013.

This emergent configuration offers several advantages to users, who get all future product updates included in their subscription, without paying additional fees. The products can be legally installed on multiple computers and mobile devices (often with restrictions on concurrent usage). They can be easily downloaded and installed on newly purchased devices without having to keep up with physical disks and serial numbers because everything is digital. Subscriptions also may include upgraded versions of cloud-based storage that are better than the free version. However, the brave new world also introduces several disadvantages. Monthly or annual subscription fees are required. If the user stops paying then the software stops working—as compared with "boxed" retail software, which can be used indefinitely once purchased. Because the products are virtual, a constant (or near-constant) Internet connection is required, so that the software can verify that the user still has a valid subscription license.

For corporate users, "software as a service" also introduces administrative complexity for software auditors. When an employee leaves the company, the firm has to ensure that company-licensed software subscriptions are no longer available to that individual. Current employees also may install personal software subscriptions on corporate machines. IT administrators may be unaware of this software, which can lead to security risks and unwanted headlines.

Offering users (like "Mike," at the beginning of the chapter) access to various applications is one way that cloud providers seek to stand out from the competition. For example, providers like Box and Dropbox operate as storage-only services. As their names imply, they are simply "boxes" into which users can dump their data. They don't offer additional software functionality options.

At the other end of the market spectrum in the cloud space, companies such as Microsoft and Adobe are leveraging existing applications that most users are likely to be familiar with—applications like Word, Excel, and Photoshop—to make their cloud offerings more appealing and to differentiate themselves in the market. Yet, Microsoft OneDrive, which integrates with the Office suite of applications, doesn't help users like Mike who may need access to Illustrator, which is an Adobe product. This kind of functional segregation between storage and software platforms (across competing entities like Microsoft and Adobe) is one of the reasons why some employees may still use unapproved cloud services, outside of the official agreements that their companies maintain with a sanctioned provider.

Reliability

While security is critical, cloud services also need to be *reliable*. Dependence on Dropbox, OneDrive, or another provider means that all of the data that a salesperson on the road, an engineer in the field, or an executive in the air may need is stored in the cloud. What happens if the cloud service is unavailable? Employees "in the office" have file backups, local file servers, or other alternate locations where their critical data are stored. If the salesperson, the engineer, the executive, or anyone on the road has been relying heavily on cloud storage, that individual is out of luck. This isn't mere post-apocalyptic fantasy. In May 2014 Adobe's Creative Cloud was offline for more than 24 hours. In 2013, Dropbox suffered two separate incidents, taking the service offline for approximately 16 hours for each event. This is a lifetime when a client is waiting for a proposal or a security code needs to be entered.

If a company is paying for cloud services, the service-level agreement (SLA) often will include an uptime guarantee (typically 99.9 percent or more). The agreement may include financial compensation in the event of breach of warranty. This compensation can help to offset productivity losses incurred by downtime, but it can do little to repair damaged reputations when the salesperson, the engineer, or the executive drops the ball for a clamoring client. For free / consumer-focused cloud services, of course, there is no such uptime guarantee. A freelancer or small business that depends on Dropbox or iCloud Drive may lose productivity and income when services go down, and get nothing in return except lost business.

Accessibility

As a point of functional definition, cloud computing depends on a nearly constant Internet connection. If a connection is unreliable, or goes down completely, the cloud model can't work. What operational concessions need to be made for users on the road or in remote locations where Internet access is uncertain? When accessing cloud-stored data from "the road"—hotels, coffee shops, convention centers, etc.—it is also essential to consider the security of the wireless network being used. If the Wi-Fi network at the convention center, for example, is open to all attendees, some of these are likely to be competitors with interest in your data! Best practice avoids leaving proprietary corporate data vulnerable over an open wireless network. Many organizations use a VPN (virtual private network) service to secure data transmission when employees are away from the office. For individual users, like caution is advisable. Don't open your tax records or other private financials stored in the cloud from an open Wi-Fi network. It is bad practice. We offer detailed discussion of wireless network security and VPN usage in Chapter 5.

What Should You Do?

As with any new device or service that has a broad range of functionalities that may or may not be germane to your needs, it is important to think about how and why you need to use a cloud service. Valid reasons for using cloud-based storage may include as a backup to your computer(s) and device(s). The cloud offers a convenient way to increase the likelihood that a blue screen of death or a "dropped-in-the-toilet" moment won't mean the loss of all of your data. The cloud also offers increased access to data across multiple locations and devices and a way to share files with colleagues, friends, and family. It is just much easier to share data on the cloud than with conventionally anchored tools.

Given the importance of maintaining the integrity of your files, it is critical to take the time to do some research on the reliability, security, and offerings available through various service providers. For most users, this kind of digging into company backgrounds to figure out the best cloud service provider probably seems complicated (and time consuming). Even if you did do some poking around on your own, there's no guarantee you'd find anything useful or that you'd be able to determine what information was the most pertinent for this purpose. Third-party media sources, such as *Consumer Reports*, *PCWorld*, *MacWorld*, and CNET.com, that regularly and objectively review a wide range of these services can be extremely useful when sorting through background issues that are important to consider before choosing a provider.

The way you use the cloud can directly impact how well protected your data are. Be extremely careful using any kind of cloud service from public computers or over public networks or open wireless networks. You should seriously consider *not* accessing any of your sensitive data from public computers or over open networks. The risk is real. If the data are important, accessing them in this way is just not smart policy.

The structure of the data storage system also is critical for maintaining the integrity of your data. Many providers maintain a "public" folder where you can easily stash files or send links to someone to whom you want to give access to those files. Although these folders are extremely convenient, someone you don't intend to could just as easily gain access to your data. A critical rule of thumb is if you don't intend for a file to be public, don't put it in the public folder!

For most (if not all) of us who work for someone else, operating within the rules of your firm's Information Security (IS) policies serves several essential (perhaps universal) goals: safeguard internal communications, protect clients' data, maintain employees' privacy, limit competitor threats. The structure of virtual systems is inherently porous and vulnerable. It is critical to be aware of—and operate according to—your company's cloud data storage policies. If your company prohibits the storage of work-related data on the cloud, don't do it! If your company offers in-house cloud storage (which is increasingly the norm in larger firms with a professional, full-time IT staff), or has an exclusive formal contract with a cloud provider, use that "official" provider.

If you use commercial cloud services, you will often receive communications intended to increase the security of your data. Although tempting, don't spam-filter these e-mails or texts; they likely contain relevant information on the services you're using. Pay attention to news reports on cloud security or cloud breaches. If you hear that your provider has suffered a data breach, or that it's been hacked, immediately change your password. It's also important, periodically, to review the data you've stored on the cloud, and remove files you no longer need to store there. Don't just "stash and forget."

Additional Reading

For more on how to navigate the cloud, see the following links, and visit our web site at www.10donts.com/cloud:

- NetworkWorld, "5 Tips to Keep Your Data Secure on the Cloud," a broad overview of cloud safety: www.networkworld.com/article/2172750/cloud-computing/5-tips-to-keep-your-data-secure-on-the-cloud.html

- Computerworld, "5 Online Backup Services Keep Your Data Safe," with advice on keeping your critical data duplicated off-site: www.computerworld.com/s/article/9223805/5_online_backup_services_keep_your_data_safe

- Forbes, "Why the Cloud Is a Safe Deposit Box for Your Data," www.forbes.com/sites/sungardas/2014/04/28/why-the-cloud-is-a-safe-deposit-box-for-your-data/

- PC Magazine, "20 Top Cloud Services for Small Businesses," with detailed analysis of cloud services as they relate to business needs: www.pcmag.com/article2/0,2817,2361500,00.asp

- CNet, "OneDrive, Dropbox, Google Drive, and Box: Which Cloud Storage Service Is Right for You?," a more consumer-focused look at cloud services: www.cnet.com/news/onedrive-dropbox-google-drive-and-box-which-cloud-storage-service-is-right-for-you/

4

Don't Look for a Free Lunch

If It's Too Good to Be True...

Elizabeth is a biochemistry researcher at a small, privately owned, pharmaceuticals firm. In preparing white papers and presentations demonstrating results of her lab work for investors, clients, and other key stakeholders, Elizabeth makes extensive use of videography. This includes video of animal subjects (primarily mice) in the lab as well as from her microscope work showing cell interactions with drug compounds.

She also frequently collaborates with researchers at other institutions, which involves sharing her own—and viewing others'—research videos. While Elizabeth uses a Windows computer, many of her colleagues use Apple Macs or Linux PCs with a wide variety of video-capture and editing software, which saves files in various formats—QuickTime, MPEG-4, AVI, Windows Media, etc. As a result, Elizabeth often is unable to open—or open properly—the video files she's been sent.

To address this problem she has downloaded various free "video conversion" utilities and browser plug-ins over the years. She's done this by simply Googling the conversion process she wants and downloading the free products she finds. She often has to go through several before finding one that does what she needs. Often, Elizabeth is unable to convert any videos with these products.

Many of these "freeware" products come with toolbars automatically installed in her browser, extra programs running in her task bar, and extraneous icons on her desktop. This extra cruft is often called "adware," "bloatware," or, less generously, "crapware." Eventually, these additional programs lead to a substantial performance drain on Elizabeth's PC, and she reports this to her IT Help Desk. The staff informs Elizabeth that there are several malware variants on her computer and some less-dangerous adware threats. They recommend that her computer be reimaged and returned to its initial state, which will cost Elizabeth and her research team substantial downtime.

Software—Consider the Source

As the way we work today increasingly depends on collaboration with others, often at a distance, software solutions to these progressively common 21st-century work arrangements have proliferated. "Peer-to-peer" (commonly referred to as "P2P") file-sharing systems can represent a legitimate network protocol. These systems offer an efficient way to share files directly from one computer to another, without going through an intermediate server. This decreases system complexity and can increase operational performance.

In the late 1990s, "P2P" morphed from a generic term describing a legitimate method of network data transmission into a specific term for illegal file sharing, most notably by users of Napster. In its original incarnation, operating from 1999 to 2001, Napster used software that made it very simple for average users to share digital music files (MP3 files). The interface also had an extremely robust search option. This differentiated Napster from previous file-sharing software focused toward more technical users. Because of the easy-to-use interface and coherent underlying structure, Napster was extremely popular during its brief existence, with an apex of more than 26 million users.

Napster was exceptionally popular on college campuses, where students often had access to high-speed Internet in their dormitories. But in 2000 several music artists (Metallica and Dr. Dre, among others), record labels, and the Recording Industry Association of America (RIAA) filed concurrent lawsuits against Napster, alleging that the service directly facilitated copyright infringement. Napster was liable because it wasn't a "true" P2P service. Napster actually maintained a central server with a virtual index of the data hosted on the "peers" in the network. The RIAA famously sued many end users: the "peers" in this system. For several years, college students, children, grandparents, single mothers, and college professors were under threat of legal action.

Following the initial slate of legal actions, a US Appeals Court ruled that Napster could remain active only if it tracked downloads on its network and immediately restricted access to copyrighted materials. This proved to be technically insurmountable, and Napster shut its "doors" in July 2001, filing for bankruptcy in 2002. The Napster name was subsequently resurrected by a legitimate pay-to-download music service. Similar services, such as Pandora, iTunes Radio, and Spotify, now offer users the ability to stream an essentially unlimited catalog of music on their devices for a minimal annual subscription fee—often $20 or less. The emergence—and broad adoption—of this nominal-fee service model, coupled with the widespread availability of broadband Internet access for streaming audio content, may have diminished the market appeal of piracy as a vehicle to access free music.

Several other pseudo P2P services, including Gnutella, LimeWire, Kazaa, and eDonkey, sprang up in Napster's wake. Although the original focus of these services was music, as Internet speeds increased and more private users could afford wide-pipe access, video files and software applications became a larger part of the business. These various services (and their users!) have been targeted by lawsuits since the early 21st century, and many have functionally ceased to exist.

Broadly, the term "warez" (pronounced "wares") has been used to describe media or other software downloaded by end users without cost over the Internet. Warez can include applications, pornography, or other media such as music or movie files. Video games are among the most frequently "pirated" applications. As the virtual infrastructure into which all private and consumer data are embedded becomes more porous, software companies have sought various remedies and copy-protection methods to prevent the widespread pirating of their products and intellectual property.

For companies like Microsoft and Adobe, one advantage of the subscription-based model they've increasingly adopted (see Chapter 3) is that their products aren't as susceptible to piracy or unauthorized use as retail or "boxed" software. Many modern warez distribution sites use the "BitTorrent" protocol. With BitTorrent, small pieces of the desired file are hosted at various sites (called "torrents") worldwide, which are reassembled when users download the target file. The Pirate Bay, based in Sweden, is currently the largest and best-known BitTorrent directory. It has, however, been the target of repeated lawsuits for copyright infringement and other intellectual property violations.

Despite these legal challenges the Pirate Bay remains in active operation. The site has relocated its servers to other countries several times to avoid legal repercussions but primarily operates from Sweden. In light of potential legal vulnerability associated with trading in illegally procured content, some US-based firms such as Facebook and Microsoft now block messages on their services that include links to Pirate Bay torrents.

Issues with Warez

Although questions of intellectual property have become much more complicated with the emergence of an infrastructure that inherently dilutes conventional ownership boundaries, legal precedent has emerged. As an initial foundational caution, downloading warez can be illegal. Doing so can put employees in explicit violation of the terms of their company's software agreement. It can also represent a violation of an employer's IT policy or a customer's agreement with an in-home Internet service provider. Any of these breaches of contract can have a wide range of negative personal, financial, and legal consequences.

Downloading or installing, for free, a retail software product that is not free is always a bad idea. Commercial firms can be—and frequently are—randomly audited by the Business Software Alliance (BSA). Terminated or disgruntled employees also occasionally report their own (or former) employer to the BSA as a form of "payback." If a company is found to be in violation of any of the explicit terms of agreement it holds with service providers, the firm as a whole can be held responsible. The illegal activities of individual employees using company systems and network resources to break the law can put the entire company in legal jeopardy.

Legal vulnerability isn't the only danger associated with warez. "Malware" is software that is designed to achieve some malicious intent that users did not intend to install (and are likely unaware has been installed) on their computer. Warez have become a very common vehicle facilitating an epidemic diffusion of malware. There are a number of broad categories of malware that users can find their machines infected with following a warez download; these have a range of unpleasant to potentially devastating consequences.

The malware may be designed to steal users' financial data. Once installed, the software can systematically attempt to capture credit card numbers, banking information, and other sensitive financial information stored on the device, or from a network accessed using that device. The malware also may be designed to obtain the user's credentials using the dictionary (or other) password attacks discussed in detail in Chapter 2. Obviously, criminals with stealth access to users' passwords can do untold damage, and this may be one of the first steps in developing an Advanced Persistent Threat (APT) attack.

Along a more aggressive tack, which is likely to be quite surprising to some readers of this book, the malware may take the form of "ransomware." For example, 2013's "CryptoLocker" was malware designed to hijack the user's computer. Once activated the program locked all of the users' files, which would remain locked until the user paid a ransom for release from the snare (discussed further in Chapter 9). Malware doesn't necessarily have a user-specific goal. It may be designed to turn a user's computer into a "bot," which is a computer controlled by an attacker. The "bot" can be used to spread malware to additional users, or to perform other malicious activities on the attacker's behalf. Outside of having any "useful" goal—if only to the criminals themselves—malware may simply be designed to be destructive, with no benefits to the attacker aside from malicious satisfaction. What's clear is that malware has a range of consequences, none of which are beneficial to end users.

Hidden Agenda

Users like "Elizabeth" looking for a tool to help translate videos from one format to another take for granted that software claiming to achieve this purpose in fact does what it claims, but this is a very dangerous assumption in the wilds of the Internet in the land of "free" software. It is much more realistic to assume that warez more frequently than not misrepresent their true contents. A download link claiming to be "Adobe Photoshop CS6-freeversion.exe" may in reality be something else entirely or (and more likely) contain hidden attacks that can fundamentally compromise your machine or network. Warez sites often lead users down a familiar series of pages, such as "click here to download," then "accept our agreement," then "download our file manager," etc. In the end, users wind up having installed several miscellaneous programs and still don't obtain the program or tool they'd been searching for in the first place!

In some instances, warez sites are specifically designed to capture end users' personal information. Users are asked for a name and e-mail address, possibly even a credit card number with the assurance "but you won't be charged!" The broad purpose of these sites is purely to mine end users' data. These are added to a database that can then be used for potentially (likely) malicious purposes.

Warez sites will often attempt a process to first trick and then infect users. With this two-step process users download a file that appears to be a trial/free/time-limited version of the application as a "hook," which snares them in a trap. The warez site then instructs users to download a "key generator" or "keygen," which then supposedly gives users a serial number for the software that can be used to activate the full version. These keygens easily can be (and frequently are) infected with vicious malware. Traditionally, pornography had been the most frequent conduit for the launch of malware. Some security experts now believe that warez, or illegal software downloads, pose more of a risk to end users than porn.[1] There may be substantially greater risk (up to 800 percent) of malware being triggered with a key generator than being embedded in porn.

Lesser Threats

While many of the mechanical consequences of malware infection are potentially devastating, others more aptly fall under the category of "annoyance" than "attack." These lesser threats include the applications, add-ons, and plug-ins that collectively have come to be known as "adware" or "bloatware." Examples of bloatware include a toolbar added to your browser claiming to offer local shopping deals, one-click access to your weather forecast, or a faster Internet search

---

[1]State of Security, Brent Huston, "Opinion: Warez More Dangerous Than Porn," http://stateofsecurity.com/?p=1282, January 28, 2011.

(which may actually be a targeted search that takes users to sites preferred by the developer). Like the example of Elizabeth at the beginning of this chapter, serious performance degradation on a computer can be attributed to the add-ons, plug-ins, and other unwanted "extras" that infected many downloads.

Applications that run on your desktop, installed with software to run a peripheral such as a printer, are also examples of bloatware. These unrelated (or vaguely related) applications may claim to offer cloud-based photo-sharing services, deals on the purchase of printer ink, or other targeted marketing. We're all tempted to click through installation instructions without reading the fine print or looking to see which boxes are checked. These steps take valuable extra time, but whenever you install any new software onto one of your devices, it is essential to consider each screen carefully. This is the only way to decrease the probability that you'll inadvertently install items other than those that you truly want and need. The more attention that you pay at the point of install, the less likely it is that you'll end up with parasites infesting your machine.

Bloatware, unlike malware, often is installed by legitimate hardware or software manufacturers to coincide with authorized retail purchases. Many new PCs purchased through retail channels will include any number of these preloaded bloatware applications. The application developer actually pays a per-install fee to the PC maker for the privilege of having its apps preinstalled for unsuspecting retail customers. End users can uninstall this software, but they often don't know what is necessary and what is not, and so leave things as they were at the time of purchase. Even if users do know what to keep and what to discard, uninstalling bloatware can be quite time-consuming.

Legitimate software downloads often include "optional" add-ons unrelated to the desired software, and which add no functionality. For example, for years the Oracle Corporation has bundled third-party products including the Ask.com browser toolbar and McAfee Security Scan with downloads of its Java software. End users can choose to opt out of these kinds of planted installs but frequently don't because the choice is an opt *out*. By default (and design!) the "accept" boxes are already checked. Typical users who simply click all the boxes labeled "Next" while installing software get extra apps that they probably didn't want or need. This practice hasn't gone unnoticed by users. Oracle has been roundly criticized for its shady bundling. As of June 2014 more than 18,000 users had signed a petition at Change.org to get Oracle to stop bundling bloatware applications with Java in this way.[2] This kind of deceptive practice often is referred to as a "drive-by download." A drive-by can use the opt in by default method, as Oracle does, but deceptive bundlers may use different methods, misrepresenting a download link on their web page as a "close this window" or other button.

---

[2]Change.org, "Oracle Corporation: Stop Bundling Ask Toolbar with the Java Installer," www.change.org/petitions/oracle-corporation-stop-bundling-ask-toolbar-with-the-java-installer.

This kind of clearly deceptive practice, where manufacturers actively seek to trick users into downloading software they had no intention of downloading, has infected the mobile device application markets as well. This particular class of parasitic infestation has been a substantially larger issue in the Windows app store than in either the Apple or Android marketplaces.[3] In fact, Google has adopted an extremely aggressive stance in defiance of these types of subversive apps in the Android marketplace. Google has explicitly adjusted its developer policies in order to effectively prohibit drive-by downloads and deceptive app descriptions.[4]

It is very easy to accidentally download a camouflaged program. Users who search on a particular term can find literally dozens of other apps that are positioned to trade on a well-known name. These "fake apps" often claim that they will help users download the real app, or will provide tips and tricks for using it, for a price. To reiterate the point, whenever you download any app, it is always best practice to get it directly from the source. If you need to download Apple's iTunes, but you aren't sure if you have a legitimate link, go to apple.com so you can eliminate all doubt. This holds for any app you're looking for. Always try to find the "official" page for an app or a program with a well-known name. That is the only way to be sure that you're actually getting what you're looking for.

How to Protect Yourself

Readers are likely to be disappointed here, but the most practical, robust first step is to simply avoid visiting warez sites looking for a chimerical "free lunch." There is no free lunch out there. If you need retail software either you (or your company) should pay for it and license it properly. Elizabeth, our biochemistry researcher, should have talked with her IT staff, her supervisor, and/or other colleagues about getting legitimate access to the software she needed through legitimate channels.

Many software manufacturers offer free versions of their software or a trial period to take a test drive. Aside from these discount periods, if you are getting access to paid software without paying for it, you are simply asking for trouble. Elizabeth could have gone this route, taking advantage of trial versions of legitimate software obtained from legitimate web sites before making a purchase—even doing this iteratively, sampling a number of options.

---

[3]How-To Geek.com, Chris Hoffman, "The Windows Store Is a Cesspool of Scams—Why Doesn't Microsoft Care?" www.howtogeek.com/194993/the-windows-store-is-a-cesspool-of-scams-why-doesnt-microsoft-care/, August 17, 2014.

[4]Naked Security, John Zorabedian, "Google Takes Aim at Deceptive Advertising of Play Store Apps," http://nakedsecurity.sophos.com/2014/04/04/google-takes-aim-at-deceptive-advertising-of-play-store-apps/ April 4, 2014.

It is important to remember that you're not locked into a particular product if it doesn't work for you. If you download a piece of software and it turns out not to function as advertised or doesn't meet your expectations, get rid of it! There is no reason to keep software on your machine that you're not going to use or that doesn't work the way you want it to. Even if it's not malware that you're contending with, or something else dangerous, it may be taking up valuable space on your hard drive or your mobile device. If you have concerns about the process of physically eliminating software from your devices, get help. Don't get stuck with something you don't want just because you're not sure how to get rid of it.

Along a similar and potentially equally dangerous track, don't try to find ways to obtain other for-purchase media such as music, movies, or mobile apps for free. Not only is it very likely to be illegal in your state, but it also puts your devices and the networks to which they're connected at serious risk.

At the other end of the spectrum, when installing legitimate retail software that you've purchased, read the included license information. You should also read the installation instructions very carefully. Uncheck any boxes for add-ons and extras that you don't need or want. Modern browsers, antivirus programs, and anti-malware software, if properly installed, may offer users warnings about drive-by and other malicious downloads. For example, Internet Explorer versions 8 and higher offer a "SmartScreen" filter that checks against a Microsoft-maintained database of unsafe content and warns users when a web site or download may be malicious (see Figure 4-1). When you purchase a new computer or mobile device, always examine the base of installed software so you know what you should have and what you shouldn't. Remove any applications, browser plug-ins, or other software that you don't need or want, which can only slow you down.

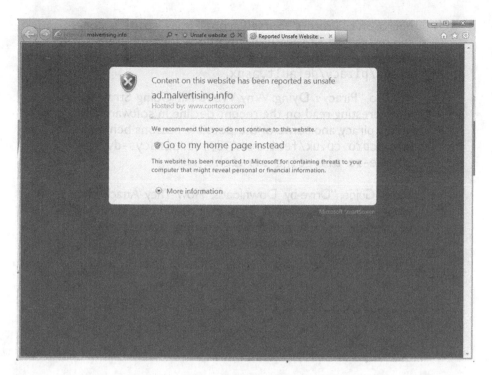

Figure 4-1. In Internet Explorer 8 and all later versions, an end user is warned if the site visited is in Microsoft's "unsafe content" database

Additional Reading

For more on the risks of illegitimate software, see the following links, and visit our web site at www.10donts.com/software:

- Business Software Alliance (BSA), a business-focused trade group web site with tips on how employers can protect themselves from the risks of unlicensed software and how to properly document software purchases: www.bsa.org/.

- Google, "Android Developers: Spam and Placement in the Store," an interesting read on the types of advertising Google's app developers can and cannot use when describing their apps: https://support.google.com/googleplay/android-developer/answer/2985717?hl=en.

- Microsoft's "Protect Yourself from Piracy" page, a consumer-focused site featuring methods for end users to determine software legitimacy: `www.microsoft.com/en-us/piracy/default.aspx`.

- PC Pro, "Piracy's Dying: Why We're All Going Straight," an interesting read on the recent decline in software and media piracy, and some of the possible reasons behind it: `www.pcpro.co.uk/features/387742/piracys-dying-why-we-re-all-going-straight`.

- Tom's Guide, "Drive-by Downloads: How They Attack and How to Defend Yourself," a good overview on the methods of infection by and preventive behaviors against drive-by downloads: `www.tomsguide.com/us/drivebydownload,news-18329.html`.

Don't Do Secure Things from Insecure Places

Location, Location, Location…

Tom is a senior sales associate for Magnatec Inc. (MTec), a large, US-based business-to-business (B2B) electrical parts supplier. He has current customers in 42 of 50 states and the potential for customers in all 50. Not surprisingly, Tom spends a great deal of his time on the road making sales calls to potential customers and servicing current customers. MTec has assigned him the typical road warrior "tools of the trade"—a laptop, tablet, and smartphone. All of Tom's gear is preconfigured by his corporate IT department. Tom takes advantage of Internet access wherever he happens to find himself: hotel rooms, coffee shops, customer conference rooms, fast-food restaurants, public restrooms, etc. He is totally indiscriminant and approaches the decision to use an available Wi-Fi based solely on convenience. When he finds a reliable and fast Internet connection, Tom often has four to six hours of work to catch up on. This can include entering new sales orders, sending queries to his sales team, requesting technical support, submitting receipts for per diem reimbursements, and the like. Tom is on the road roughly 150 days a year, so he's often catching up on his personal to-do list as well. Paying bills, checking credit card statements, and sending receipts for tax purposes to his accountant are all on his list.

Tom spends little or no time considering the security of the wireless networks he uses. What's more, as readers are likely to have guessed from the description of his behavior, many of these networks are completely open, available to all of the customers at a coffee shop or the guests in a hotel at any given time. Recently, MTec introduced a virtual private network (VPN) service to more effectively protect company data in transit. MTec employees have been instructed to connect to the VPN when on the road and transmitting or receiving company data. Because connecting to the VPN requires a second (and separate) step, after connecting to Wi-Fi, Tom (along with many other MTec employees) often "forgets" or neglects that step. This puts employees' company data (and their personal data) at serious risk.

Background: Wireless Networking at Home, at Work, and on the Road

At this point, mid-way through 2014, most of us (even those who didn't grow up using the Internet in school or smartphones to surf the Web) are now extremely familiar with Wi-Fi, which has become very nearly ubiquitous in modern society. We use Wi-Fi at airports, train stations, universities, coffee shops, bars, hotels, restaurants, public parks, conference centers, public toilets, movie theaters, the stores where we shop, and in our homes and workplaces. We take it completely for granted. In our minds it is just there. We expect it to "just work," and most of the time it does. But even when it does "just work" how it's supposed to work in our minds, does it work for us in a safe, secure way?

Home Sweet Home…

At home, a wireless router or access point set up by a telecommunications provider (Comcast, AT&T, Charter, etc.) very likely uses a default username/password combination. Although the technician may or may not change these defaults at the time the system is installed, customers certainly should do exactly that! If not—if users just leave system settings unchanged—criminals can very easily take advantage of published and widely available default credentials to access users' home wireless network, and potentially their private data as well. Similarly, a router purchased through a retailer (from a manufacturer such as Linksys, Netgear, etc.) also has default factory-set credentials (see Figure 5-1). Customers who choose not to—or don't think to—change these credentials are putting themselves at risk.

Select Router Manufacturer: ROUTERS-INC ▾ [Get Password!]

Manufacturer	Model	Username	Password
ROUTERS-INC	QQ1234	admin	default
ROUTERS-INC	QQ1235	admin	(none)
ROUTERS-INC	QQ1236	administrator	admin
ROUTERS-INC	QQ1237	admin	1237

Figure 5-1. Default credentials for most brands of wireless access points and routers are freely available with a simple web search. This can be useful if a home user needs to reset a router, but it also means that users who don't reset these default passwords are vulnerable to attackers

In June 2014, Comcast ruffled some feathers with a project blurring the lines between "home" and "public" wireless networks. When subscribers to Comcast's Xfinity Internet service received new cable equipment in their home, many discovered that the device broadcasts a second, disparate wireless network called "XfinityWiFi." Comcast intends to create a nationwide network grid. This would allow Xfinity subscribers to log on to one of these wireless hotspots—though this so-called public hotspot may in reality be broadcasting from private users' homes!

Comcast allows customers to disable this feature, but the default is active. The telecom giant claims the two networks (private and public) are independent, with distinct antennas inside the hardware, and that outsiders would never have access to a customer's private devices or data. Comcast also maintains that because public Wi-Fi users have to sign in using Comcast credentials, the public users (and not the home subscribers) would be responsible for any crimes committed over the Wi-Fi network.

Despite these assurances, customers and analysts are uneasy with this arrangement. Any access, regardless of how limited it is, can be exploited. "If you're opening up another access point, it increases the likelihood that someone can tamper with your router," says Craig Young, a security researcher at Tripwire.[1]

(Using a ubiquitous public network such as "XfinityWiFi" or "ATT Wifi," so that your mobile device automatically connects to any network with that name, raises other security issues as attackers can "spoof" these network designations. We discuss this threat in greater detail in Chapter 7.)

---

[1]CNN, Jose Pagliery, "Comcast Is Turning Your Home Router into a Public Wi-Fi Hotspot," http://money.cnn.com/2014/06/16/technology/security/comcast-wifi-hotspot/, June 16, 2014.

Back at the Office. . .

In the professional sphere, most large organizations maintain a default wireless policy and lock down their Wi-Fi networks. Organizations that do not maintain proper oversight can easily find employees setting up their own wireless routers, creating "rogue" Wi-Fi networks. These rogue networks may be set up by employees when the wireless signal is poor in certain parts of the plant or in an attempt to circumvent filtering (or other restrictions) often imposed on users of wireless networks. These hotspots—physical wireless access devices—can introduce vulnerabilities to the corporate network and allow outsiders (potentially criminals seeking access for financial gain or mischief) to gain entry to the system.

It is critical that corporate network administrators regularly "sniff" their network to seek out these rogue access points and remove them from the network. Administrators can use a "WIPS" (wireless intrusion protection system) to automatically detect unauthorized access points. It is also critical to encourage or incentivize employees to resist the temptation to install or to use unapproved networks. Ultimately, introducing additional points of system vulnerability isn't good for anyone except potential attackers.

On the Road Again. . .

Challenges to system vulnerability within the context of the actual physical plant where you work vs. when you work at a distance are quite disparate. End users on the road face an entirely different set of challenges. We are all grateful when we find an open, available wireless network with good performance—"Can I get a miracle please?" But, these networks carry risks. A network with an open login is just that—*open*. It's open to everyone. An open network might be okay for checking on baseball scores, or reading headlines. These aren't personal data with any kind of inherent value to users per se; they are public data. But an open login shouldn't be used for sensitive work or personal data because doing so makes these private data public. A secure network or VPN on top of an open network (see VPN section following) should always be used for sensitive data. Otherwise, anyone can see exactly what you'd like to keep private.

Because of the almost perpetual Wi-Fi in hotels, convention centers, airports, bars, and restaurants, modern travelers' wireless connections are the focus of this chapter. Nevertheless, the same cautions also apply with "old school" wired connections. Don't do online banking or sensitive work transactions from a desktop computer in a hotel's business center, for example. Don't assume that a wired connection in a hotel room is any more secure than a wireless connection. If improperly configured, your wired traffic can be visible to other hotel guests or employees monitoring the connection.

In July of 2014, the United States Secret Service (USSS) released an advisory to the hospitality industry concerning hotel business center devices, primarily focused on desktop computers.[2] The USSS, in conjunction with the Department of Homeland Security, warned hoteliers that attackers had been caught using "keyloggers" on the business center computers in several hotels in Texas. A keylogger is a piece of software (or more infrequently a hardware device) that captures every keystroke typed on a computer keyboard. With this software installed, a criminal can capture e-mail logins, banking information, corporate credentials, or any other information entered using the keyboard. As a basic law of survival in the cyber jungle, it is simply unsafe to use publicly accessible PCs for any purpose beyond checking the weather report or football scores. This includes machines in the public library, in university computer labs, at the airport, or anywhere else that end users don't maintain autonomous, exclusive physical control of the device(s) they're using to enter, send, or manipulate sensitive data.

Encryption Standards

In tandem with the increasing ubiquity of Wi-Fi in modern society, several sophisticated encryption methods have been developed to protect end users' data from criminals seeking to steal it. The most commonly used encryption methods are sanctioned by the Institute of Electrical and Electronics Engineers (IEEE) Standards Authorization. These methods are broadly referred to as the "802.1X" standards. The first, released in 1999, was called "Wired Equivalent Privacy (WEP)." This was by any current benchmark an extremely basic standard, employing a 40-bit key (which later was increased in size to 128-bit). By the early 2000s, serious concerns had emerged as to the protection offered through WEP, based on the relative ease with which its password (or key) could be cracked by criminals seeking unauthorized access.

Even though the IEEE officially declared WEP "deprecated" as of 2004, and the FBI demonstrated in 2005 that any WEP key could be cracked in less than three minutes using commonly available retail computers and tools available for free on the Internet, some organizations continued to use it! Users were consciously choosing to ignore evidence that their network protection was faulty. As in so many areas of our lives, including personal health, finance, and romantic spheres, denial can be a very powerful driver of dangerous behavior.

In January of 2007 the retailer T.J. Maxx—a department store chain operating more than 1,000 stores in the United States and throughout the United

---

[2]Krebs on Security, Brian Krebs, "Beware Keyloggers at Hotel Business Centers," http://krebsonsecurity.com/2014/07/beware-keyloggers-at-hotel-business-centers/, July 14, 2014.

Kingdom and continental Europe—suffered a massive data breach exposing the credit card numbers of more than 45 million users to theft. A significant contributing factor underlying this breach was the attackers' access to the corporate network over the Wi-Fi in a particular store that had been using the WEP protocol. T.J. Maxx's parent corporation estimated that the breach cost over $250 million in damages.[3]

Despite substantial evidence of the inadequate protective screen offered by WEP, the Payment Card Industry (PCI), a consortium of leading banking and credit card companies, did not officially prohibit the use of the WEP protocol in financial data transmission until 2008. Perhaps most surprising here, in light of the massive security losses in which WEP had been directly complicit, existing WEP installations were "grandfathered in" until June 2010! Perhaps, to paraphrase Oscar Wilde, we really do have the power to deny anything we like.

In 2003, in response to the weakness uncovered in WEP, a "draft" version of the next IEEE 802.1X standard was released. This standard is commonly referred to as WPA, for "Wi-Fi Protected Access" (or sometimes WPA1). WPA represented a significant improvement over the older WEP protocol. WPA employed a new encryption key for each packet of data either being sent to or received by a network, rather than using a standard key for all data packets.

The new WPA protocol was embraced by savvy administrators and forward-thinking organizations aware of the weaknesses of the older WEP protocol, and applied to new web infrastructure. Older WEP routers and access points were not upgradeable to WPA technology, so organizations had to commit funds and other resources to transition their systems to WPA protection. As in the case of the widely publicized T.J. Maxx breach, many organizations delayed this upgrade in accord with the 2010 grandfather date to lower costs. The delayed transition did not go unnoticed by criminals.

In 2004, WPA2 was finalized as IEEE standard 802.11i. The emergence of WPA2 hastened the official depreciation of WEP. WPA2 used substantially stronger cryptographic keys for data encryption than previous encryption protocols. Fortunately, most WPA1 hardware was upgradeable via firmware (permanent read-only software programmed into memory) to the WPA2 standard, incurring no additional equipment costs and consequently increasing adoption rates.

In light of the widening private use of network infrastructure WPA2 was offered in two "flavors." The WPA2-Personal version was intended for home users, and employed a shared passphrase that all devices in a home or small business

---

[3]Boston.com, Ross Kerber, "Cost of Data Breach at TJX Soars to $256m," http://www.boston.com/business/articles/2007/08/15/cost_of_data_breach_at_tjx_soars_to_256m/, August 15, 2007.

network could easily share across the network. The WPA2-Enterprise version was intended for much larger corporate-scale networks. In addition to a shared "encryption key" WPA2 could be configured to require an extra logon. For example, users on a corporate network using Microsoft Active Directory could be prompted for their AD (active directory) credentials to complete the Wi-Fi network logon.

In addition, modern wireless infrastructures can be configured to require "two-factor authentication," as discussed in Chapter 2. In this scenario, a password for the wireless network has to be used with a USB token, a smart card, a fingerprint scan, a code provided by a mobile app, or additional second factor.

VPN

Wireless networks can offer informed, professional users technical signals as to the level of security present in a given network, but, except in the case of home networks, the average end user can't tell what type of security a wireless network (train station, airport, hotel, coffee shop, etc.) is using. The absence of any prompt for a password, key, or other credential of course indicates that there is *no* security present in the network whatsoever! But beyond the absence of a security prompt, average users don't know if the Wi-Fi they're on is using the WEP, WPA, WPA2, or some other security protocol. In the absence of any assurances concerning wireless security, conscientious users really have only two choices.

One, don't transmit any personal, sensitive, or work-related data over that network. This isn't as easy to avoid doing as it sounds. Often times, our mobile devices are transmitting or receiving data in the "background" when they are connected to a wireless network, with no instruction from the user intentionally prompting such data transmission activity. E-mail clients check e-mail, Facebook looks for new messages, location-aware services may be using GPS, etc. Your mobile devices may be having ongoing conversations with numerous other mobile devices of which you are simply unaware—by design. We discuss "background" wireless activity in relation to mobile devices more deeply in Chapter 7.

If complete public abstinence isn't possible, a VPN (virtual private network) is the only viable option. In the universe of confusing 21st-century computing acronyms that have begun to proliferate in public discourse, VPN actually is perfectly named (see Figure 5-2). The network is "virtual." It does not require a physical connection to corporate headquarters, or a specific geographic location. The network also is "private." In a properly configured VPN, data are encrypted at both ends of the tunnel: at origin and destination. An attacker who intercepts the data stream somewhere in the middle can see only useless gibberish; nothing of value is revealed. It is also a "network." The VPN is a secure "channel" or "tunnel" that carves through the public Internet carrying private encrypted data from sender to receiver.

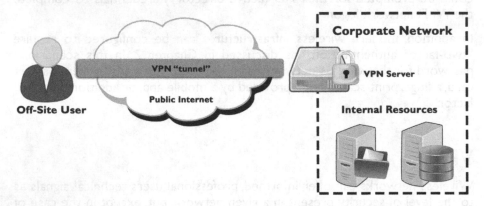

Figure 5-2. A VPN creates a private and secure "tunnel" through the public Internet

Workplace Security, on the Road

For all intents and purposes, users of a VPN should be able to do everything, with the same level of privacy and security, that they can do from their home or corporate network. Often, access to certain internal sites, databases, or file shares on a corporate network is restricted geographically, so that only devices within a certain physical distance to the server can access these resources. Universities often restrict access to online journals, or other contracted databases to users physically on campus, per the written terms of their agreements with publishers or other content providers. This kind of usage boundary often is accomplished using the Internet protocol (IP) address of the device seeking access. Here, from the standpoint of access to critical resources, an off-site device connecting via the VPN is assigned an IP address within the same range as those devices physically proximal to the university or corporate physical plant. The off-site device looks and functions via the network just as a device physically on the campus or in the building, and the user can access internal resources accordingly.

When a company mandates the use of a VPN to access corporate data or use corporate resources, the security of the user's wireless network (or even wired network, for that matter) is essentially irrelevant. If a digital resource is protected behind a VPN, users must connect to the VPN at all times whenever they are away from their physical workspace. The Internet connection type is immaterial from the standpoint of data security. VPN use isn't limited to remote users. Increasingly, organizations are beginning to use VPNs at their physical locations for certain core employees or certain critical services, as an extra step to protect their most sensitive data. Employees may not need to connect to the VPN to check their e-mail or send out a standard contract but would need to access the VPN to pull up the firm's HR database or invoice client records.

Although the use of a VPN can substantially diminish the external vulnerability associated with data sent through the pipe, interestingly, the use of a company VPN also has the potential to introduce security concerns for individual private users. An employee working away from the office connected to the VPN for work purposes may decide to send a personal non-work e-mail or execute personal financial transactions over the secure portal. In most conventional VPN configurations all of the user's traffic (work-related or other) is routed through the company's VPN server(s) while the user is connected to the network. In theory the company or other organization representatives can monitor employees' personal transactions and also access their personal credentials or other sensitive data. "Tom," from our chapter opener, didn't consistently use the VPN available to him more out of indifference or forgetfulness than anything else. But some users may approach this decision more systematically, purposefully using their employer's VPN for some but not all of their digital traffic.

This kind of inadvertent (on the user's side) internal vulnerability can emerge within what is called "full tunnel" VPN. Here, there is no mechanical segregation of data moving through the pipe. By contrast, split-tunnel VPN is designed to attempt to "intelligently" route data packets and requests. When the pipe is split, work-related packets go through the VPN server(s). Non-work-related data do not go through the protected channel, and instead are channeled through the public Internet only.

However, this kind of intelligent infrastructure is probably best thought of as being more organic in function than mechanical. Split-tunnel VPNs are at best an inexact science, and intelligent routing is far from perfect in practice. Given that both public and corporate conduits carry potential privacy liabilities, users have the option of leveraging their own VPN. Best practice in this context for end users—not withstanding issues of convenience—may be for them to connect to their corporate VPN for work-related tasks only and then reconnect to a private VPN before executing personal transactions. Yet, this can contribute to situations like Tom's, where transactions that "should" be performed over a VPN are made through vulnerable public channels. An alternative, more employer-driven approach would be for managers (or IT staff) to position all sensitive company resources behind a firewall or other infrastructure that is accessible only through the VPN. This approach simplifies the end-user decision process considerably. If someone like Tom "forgets" to connect his VPN, he won't be able to access any sensitive data!

Extra Layers of Protection

The security offered through a VPN can be enhanced when more sophisticated protocols are used to access network resources, which can include the incorporation of smart cards and tokens. As discussed in Chapter 2, increasingly, organizations are adopting a multilayered approach in what is broadly referred to as two-factor authentication. The adoption of layered protection also has become much more common for VPN connections, where users must employ a physical device (often a smart card—a credit card–sized device used to prove identity—or a USB token) in conjunction with a password to authenticate to the VPN (see Figure 5-3).

Secure Token User Authentication

Enter your token credentials

Username: [   ]

Password: [   ]

Figure 5-3. Many corporate VPN systems require two-factor authentication for login—a physical identity token or smart card and the associated PIN or password

Despite the obvious inconvenience factor associated with this more complex approach, a common rationale made for adopting a two-factor gate is that users most often connecting to firm resources through a VPN also are likely to be the "road warriors" or frequent travelers who are rarely in the office. Because of this, these also are the users most likely to lose a mobile device or have one stolen, as compared with users who work primarily in their at-work office. A stolen laptop, tablet, or smartphone, combined with a digitally stored VPN password, can allow a reasonably sophisticated thief unfettered access to sensitive company data or systems, which can have potentially lethal consequences.

Requiring employees to use a smart card or token (most of which do not allow for passwords to be saved) offers an additional line of defense that can help to thwart a potentially devastating attack. Organizations not using two-factor authentication for VPN access should be diligent in requiring employees (or other users) to immediately change their credentials in the event a device is lost or stolen.

Other Uses for VPNs

Although VPNs are most common in corporate, government, and academic environments, private end users also can benefit from the security they offer. One of the most common non-work-related applications is to disguise an end user's physical location.

For example, many live video streams, such as coverage of sporting events like the World Cup, are available only in certain countries. A stream that is just available in Germany isn't typically available to viewers in the United States. However, if an account is obtained with a German VPN provider, the sports-casting provider won't be aware of the user's true location. Game on!

Likewise, users in countries where the government filters Internet access can use a VPN to circumvent these restrictions. A user in China, for example, where Facebook is banned, may connect to a VPN to access the popular social media site. Users who leverage third-party providers (i.e., those not sponsored by their employer) should make the effort to learn their provider's privacy and security policies and not blindly trust the VPN provider with the flashiest advertising.

It's important here to remind readers what a VPN is for and what it is *not* for. A VPN can protect data in transit from snoops, and it can disguise users' physical location. While the connection between the user and the VPN is secured, the connection between the VPN provider and the user's destination may or may not be. A VPN is not designed to provide complete end-user anonymity, to prevent surveillance of browsing activities or location. We discuss methods to accomplish those goals in Chapter 6.

Additional Reading

For more on how to protect yourself in the world of Wi-Fi, see the following links, and visit our web site at www.10donts.com/wireless:

- ITWorld, "If Your Router Is Still Using the Default Password, Change It Now!" The author describes using published credentials to access several poorly protected routers: www.itworld.com/consumerization-it/326421/ if-your-router-still-using-default-password- change-it-now

- WikiHow, "How to Change Your Wi Fi Password," with definitive instructions and screenshots for most common routers: www.wikihow.com/Change-Your-Wi- Fi-Password

- Seattle PI, "Comcast Is Turning Your Xfinity Router into a Public Wi-Fi Hotspot," describing the Comcast program and how subscribers can opt out: http://blog. seattlepi.com/techblog/2014/06/09/comcast-is-turning-your-xfinity-router-into-a-public-wi-fi-hotspot/

- Lifehacker, "Why You Should Start Using a VPN (and How to Choose the Best One for Your Needs)," a good overview of VPNs with some reviewed: http://lifehacker. com/5940565/why-you-should-start-using-a-vpn-and-how-to-choose-the-best-one-for-your-needs

- PC Magazine, "10 VPN Services You Should Know About," a comprehensive review of many leading VPN services: www.pcmag.com/article2/0,2817,2403388,00.asp

Don't Let the Snoops In

Keep Your Personal Data Personal…

Maria is an attorney who specializes in issues of privacy. She advises clients on the application of encryption methods, secure transmission of data, data protection overseas, etc. She counsels corporate clients on their rights concerning information and data related to disgruntled or terminated employees, and company rights bearing on examination of employee-used laptops and other devices. On corporate-owned devices, including phones and tablets, users can have absolutely no expectation of privacy. The firm can monitor and track all employee communications—work-related and personal—and look at all of their data at will. Because of Maria's expertise in this area, her friends and family come to her with their personal privacy concerns as well. Her friends hear about current scandals and stories in the news, such as the recent Edward Snowden case, about search engines like DuckDuckGo and browsers like Tor, and ask Maria's professional opinion of these events. Although she advises them to maintain their privacy to as great an extent as possible, she also admits that the open nature of the Internet is mechanically somewhat antithetical to the maintenance of total privacy.

Maria has had many spirited discussions with her friends and family about the practice of what has come to be called "targeted advertising." Targeting is a tactic encompassing a set of tracking methods that commercial firms use to determine end users' search patterns and browsing history. These data are used to select and present ads coinciding with preferences for related products and services. Maria's opinion is that if you have to see ads on the Internet anyway, they might as well be relevant. Many of her friends disagree. They find the practice "creepy" and "Big Brother-ish," but Maria sees preference matching more as being consistent with the nature of the Internet in the 21st century. Information about us is everywhere.

Who Are the "Snoops"?

When educated, professional, up-to-date consumers today hear the words "snoops" or "spies," they are most likely to think of government encroachment on privacy and civil liberties. In the United States we tend to think in terms of the most famous (or perhaps infamous) "three-letter agencies": the NSA (National Security Agency), FBI (Federal Bureau of Investigation), and CIA (Central Intelligence Agency). Other countries have very similar agencies pursuing national security agendas, such as the GCHQ in the United Kingdom and the Mossad in Israel. In the United States, since 2001, it's become increasingly evident that the NSA in particular has extremely broad access to a great deal of personal and financial data on ordinary American citizens.

This agency has access to data from our phone calls, text messages, e-mails, web site visits, social media posts, etc. Such data include not only information at the "to whom the call was made" or "from whom an e-mail was received" level, known as metadata, but content-related data as well—deep, personal content. The NSA "mines" the data and then subjects them to profound analysis using mathematical algorithms and artificial intelligence to uncover underlying patterns. These patterns are used to elicit usable information on people who may be involved with terrorist groups or other suspect organizations. The legality of this kind of data mining, often focused on citizens who have neither been accused nor convicted of a crime, without a specific court warrant, has been and continues to be hotly debated in courtrooms in the United States, United Kingdom, and around the world. An in-depth discussion of the legal issues bearing on this topic is well outside the scope of this book. Nonetheless, the accumulation, analysis, and application of personal data by governmental entities are raising serious civil liberties concerns that are likely to have far-reaching policy implications once the dust begins to settle on these questions. As of now, these implications are unclear.

The legality of governments spying on their own citizens is in doubt and calls into question a wide range of deeply held beliefs reflective of our identity as citizens in the Land of the Free, but of course countries do not limit their "snooping" activities to their own citizens. In 2013 the French newspaper Le Monde released a damning report accusing the NSA of collecting the telephone conversations and text messages of over 70 million French citizens. Caitlin Hayden, then spokeswoman for the National Security Council, responded: "The United States gathers foreign intelligence of the type gathered by all nations. We've begun to review the way that we gather intelligence, so that we properly balance the legitimate security concerns of our citizens and allies with the privacy concerns that all people share." This doesn't all go one way—it works in the other direction too. In May 2014, a US grand jury indicted five Chinese military officers, charging them with espionage and cyber crimes related to attacks at six US corporations. The Chinese government, which maintains no formal extradition policy with the United States, has flatly refused to hand over these officials to face trial.

Of course, on everyone's radar is the highly electric case of Edward Snowden, which has generated an enormous level of media attention on the issues of privacy and government snooping. A former NSA contractor, Snowden released thousands of classified documents to the media in June 2013, fled to Russia, and was granted asylum in August 2013. The documents leaked by Snowden revealed the existence of many ominous US and worldwide surveillance programs.

These programs include the following:

- Boundless Informant
- PRISM
- Tempora
- MUSCULAR
- FASCIA
- Dishfire
- Optic Nerve

Let's take a closer look at them now.

Boundless Informant

This is a big data mining and analysis tool used by the NSA. The documents leaked by Snowden included a "heat map" (shown in Figure 6-1) depicting the density of the NSA's relative surveillance levels worldwide. Writing for the *Wire*, columnist Philip Bump estimated that this program gathered 9.7 petabytes of information (equal to 970,000 gigabytes) in a single month.[1]

---

[1]*Wire*, Philip Bump, "How Big Is the NSA Police State, Really?" www.thewire.com/national/2013/06/nsa-datacenters-size-analysis/66100/, June 11, 2013.

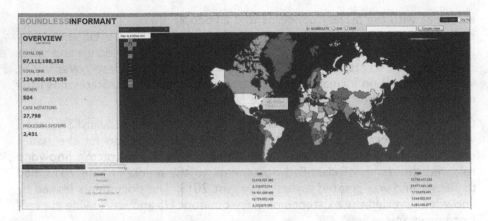

Figure 6-1. This "heat map," part of the NSA's Boundless Informant program, shows the relative levels of surveillance performed on countries worldwide. Countries in green have relatively few surveillance actions, while countries in yellow, orange, and red, are more closely watched. (Public domain image, prepared by a US government official.)

PRISM

This is an electronic surveillance program started by the NSA in 2007 that gathers stored e-mails and other Internet communications from companies like Google, Verizon, and Yahoo!. This program takes advantage of the fact that much of the world's Internet communication passes through servers in the United States (see Figure 6-2), even when neither sender nor recipient are physically in the United States.

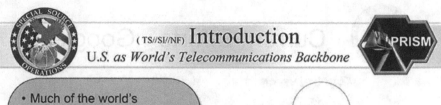

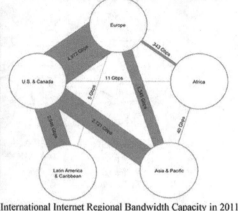

Figure 6-2. A presentation slide from the NSA's PRISM surveillance program shows how data may be captured from servers inside the United States, even when the destination and recipient are in other countries. (Public domain image, prepared by a US government official.)

Tempora

Tempora is a British Government Communications Headquarters (GCHQ) surveillance program whose data are regularly shared with the US government. This program uses secret taps on the fiber-optic backbone cables that undergird the Internet.

MUSCULAR

MUSCULAR is a joint US/UK program designed to access e-mail, documents, and mapping data from Google and Yahoo! (see Figure 6-3). Documents released by Snowden claimed that the MUSCULAR program had accessed millions of records at Google and Yahoo!.

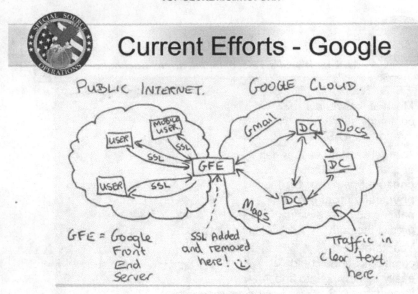

Figure 6-3. Documents released by Edward Snowden claimed that the MUSCULAR program had accessed large amounts of customer data at Google and Yahoo! by exploiting the servers connecting these companies' private networks to the public Internet. According to the Washington Post, "Two engineers with close ties to Google exploded in profanity when they saw [this] drawing."[2] (Public domain image, prepared by a US government official.)

FASCIA

This is an NSA database that collects geolocation data (i.e., physical location) from cell phones, tablets, laptops, and other electronic devices.

Dishfire

Dishfire is a second joint US/UK program designed to collect text messages from users worldwide, analyzing them using an algorithm-driven tool called Prefer.

---

[2]*Washington Post*, Barton Gellman and Ashkan Soltani, "NSA Infiltrates Links to Yahoo, Google Data Centers Worldwide, Snowden Documents Say," www.washingtonpost. com/world/national-security/nsa-infiltrates-links-to-yahoo-google-data-centers-worldwide-snowden-documents-say/2013/10/30/e51d661e-4166-11e3-8b74-d89d714ca4dd_story.html, October 30, 2013.

Optic Nerve

This is a GCHQ program developed in conjunction with the NSA that collects webcam still-images from users without their knowledge. This program was first publicly disclosed in February 2014. Documents released by Snowden indicate that the program was active from 2008 until at least 2012. The Snowden documents revealed that users were viewed from their own webcams and were "unselected," or randomly chosen. An ACLU statement offered that "This is a truly shocking revelation that underscores the importance of the debate on privacy now taking place and the reforms being considered. In a world in which there is no technological barrier to pervasive surveillance, the scope of the government's surveillance activities must be decided by the public, not secretive spy agencies interpreting secret legal authorities."

So, Who Else Is Snooping?

The NSA, FBI, CIA, and other "three-letter agencies" definitely receive the most press attention when it comes to invasions of personal privacy and Internet eavesdropping. Snooping, however, is in no way limited to governments monitoring our telephone conversations or cataloging our text messages. Other agencies and groups have a vested (financial) interest in collecting as much data as they can about end users' Internet activities, and, critical here, it may not be in those users' best interest to allow this kind of access to their private activities.

For-Profit Corporations

For-profit corporations are very interested in you—and your money—and want to know what you spend your time searching for online. If you are looking at products manufactured or sold by a competitor, businesses want to know about it. They want to display advertisements relevant to your online searches, with the goal of helping you to realize that their products or services are better and that you should purchase from them rather than the competition.

Consistent with the online omnipresence theme, in June 2014 the social media giant Facebook announced that it would begin tracking users' browsing habits outside of Facebook.com or the mobile Facebook app. If users are logged in to Facebook while browsing other sites online, Facebook would use those search data to guide its display of ads to coincide with the content of users' online activity. "The thing that we have heard from people is that they want more targeted advertising," said Brian Boland, Facebook's vice president in charge of ads product marketing. "The goal is to make it clear to people why they saw the ad."[3] Market research firm Qriously, in a recent study commissioned by the *Wall Street Journal*'s CMO Today, reported that the privacy question may simply be a matter of semantics. Qriously announced that 54 percent of the respondents in their research said that they preferred "relevant" ads to "irrelevant" ads. The preferences of "Maria" from the beginning of the chapter may be among the majority. Yet, in the same survey, only 48 percent preferred "targeted" ads to "non-targeted" ads. Here, "relevant" and "targeted" are actually the same concept phrased differently. Users apparently don't likely to feel "targeted," even if they are![4]

Employers

Although the government serves at the discretion of the people, theoretically, and for-profit organizations exist only as a consequence of market whimsy, most of us work for employers who do have legitimate claims on where we go and how we spend our time online. Employers have a vested interest in keeping track of what their employees do when they are using company equipment. Equipment can include computers, tablets, smartphones, company wireless networks, and any other infrastructure that supports employees' online activities. The rights of employers to essentially unfettered access to all of our data and information have been upheld in a wide range of contexts. In the United States, courts have consistently ruled that employees have no "expectation of privacy" in the workplace.[5,6]

In light of this access, it is critical that employers maintain a comprehensive acceptable use policy (AUP) for company IT resources, with the penalties associated with violations of the policy clearly articulated. It is more critical that employees follow these policies!

---

[3]*New York Times*, Vindu Goel, "Facebook to Let Users Alter Their Ad Profiles," www.nytimes.com/2014/06/13/technology/facebook-to-let-users-alter-their-ad-profiles.html?_r=1, June 12, 2014.

[4]*Wall Street Journal*, Jack Marshall, "Do Consumers Really Want Targeted Ads?" http://blogs.wsj.com/cmo/2014/04/17/do-consumers-really-want-targeted-ads/, April 17, 2014.

[5]American Bar Association, Diane Vaksdal Smith and Jacob Burg, "What Are the Limits of Employee Privacy?" www.americanbar.org/publications/gp_solo/2012/november_december2012privacyandconfidentiality/what_are_limits_employee_privacy.html, November/December 2012.

[6]Wolters Kluwer Employment Law Daily, Ron Miller, "Employees Have No Reasonable Expectation to Privacy for Materials Viewed or Stored on Employer-Owned Computers or Servers," www.employmentlawdaily.com/index.php/2011/11/24/employees-have-no-reasonable-expectation-to-privacy-for-materials-viewed-or-stored-on-employer-owned-computers-or-servers/, November 24, 2011.

Given the increasingly flimsy boundaries separating personal from work spaces, these policies may carry over into employees' personally owned devices. This kind of restriction/penalty carryover is most likely when employees' own equipment is used to access work resources or to connect to company networks. The main issue in focus throughout this book is control over the loss or theft of data. Employees often are compelled by AUPs to report the theft or loss of any electronic device—whether it be their company's or their own—used to access company resources. Failure to report this kind of loss can be significant. Broad-scale compromise of virtual infrastructure, the loss or theft of clients' personal data, competitor access to trade secrets, and even employment termination are potential consequences of noncompliance. It also is now extremely common practice among many larger firms to require the use of a pass-code or PIN on employees' personal mobile devices before connection to corporate e-mail servers is permitted.

■ **Note** This requirement, and its benefits, will be discussed further in Chapter 7.

Where Your Data Are...

Keeping the snoops out of your data involves different kinds of approaches depending on whether the focus is "data at rest" or "data in transit." Data at rest refers to data stored on any one of a user's personal devices, such as photos, tax documents, or work-related spreadsheets on a hard drive, the flash memory in a phone or tablet, etc. Those same data often need to be sent to, or are received from, someone else as work-related materials are forwarded for a meeting or pictures sent to a family member; they then become "data in transit."

Data on the Move

When your data are on the move, there are some steps that can be taken to protect them on your own device(s). But users have to rely on third-party providers or employers to protect these data in transit. For example, end users can take advantage of products such as PGP (Pretty Good Privacy) to digitally sign their e-mails. If PGP is used then e-mails can be read only if the recipient has a "key" to access them. This key can be provided over the phone or through other non-e-mail methods. However, both using and configuring PGP is technically complex. Likely as a result of this complexity it has not seen widespread adoption. Somewhat famously, journalist Glenn Greenwald nearly lost his chance to initiate contact with Edward Snowden because he couldn't get PGP correctly configured.[7]

In June 2014 Google announced that it had begun testing a plug-in for its Chrome browser. When used in conjunction with Gmail services this "end-to-end" plug-in is intended to make the e-mail encryption/decryption process much simpler for end users. This is likely to increase its visibility over more complex options, including PGP. Other similar encryption programs, such as "miniLock," are starting to appear in the marketplace, focused on a wider, nontechnical audience.

In addition to e-mail, many people also adopt cloud services to move their data. While most of these services claim some level of encryption of customers' data in transit (diminishing the probability that third-party attackers can gain access to it), many also reserve the right to inspect users' data or provide access to these data to authorities if requested. However, providers' dependence on governmental license to engage in interstate commerce increases the complexity of their relationship with your data as it pertains to issues of privacy.

For example, in 2012 Microsoft suspended the accounts of a SkyDrive (now OneDrive) customer because he had uploaded data that violated terms of usage, even though the data in question were for his own private use and not shared with other users. In Microsoft's terms of use[8] there are prohibitions against material that "depicts nudity of any sort including full or partial human nudity or nudity in non-human forms such as cartoons, fantasy art or manga" or "incites, advocates, or expresses pornography, obscenity, vulgarity, profanity, hatred, bigotry, racism, or gratuitous violence." With the emergence of such morality policing, items (images, sound files, videos) entirely legal to own, and unshared with other users, can put users in violation of the terms of service for a cloud provider such as Microsoft. What this also means is that cloud providers are (presumably periodically) scanning users' files for potential violations of their terms of service. Big Brother is watching, even if you're paying.

Some lesser-known cloud services—Wuala (wuala.com), SpiderOak (spideroak.com), and Tresorit (tresorit.com), for example—require users to encrypt all of their files before uploading any data to their storage services. Because the data encryption is performed on the user's local devices (and only users know the encryption password) these providers couldn't examine customers' data even if they wanted to. Perhaps more important is that if

---

[7]*Wired*, Andy Greenberg, "The Ultra-Simple App That Lets Anyone Encrypt Anything," www.wired.com/2014/07/minilock-simple-encryption/, July 3, 2014.
[8]Windows, http://windows.microsoft.com/en-GB/windows-live/code-of-conduct, April 2009.

"required" to make these files available to formal authorities or government agencies, they would be inaccessible. It is possible that the size/reputation vs. data sanctity trade-off will shift market sentiment toward smaller, less established providers that functionally eliminate the content vulnerability variable from the services purchase equation. Time will tell.

Taking an Active Role in Protecting Your Data

The industry is not ignoring the extent that operational considerations bearing on privacy coincide with market sentiment. In November 2013 the Electronic Frontier Foundation (EFF) began surveying Internet companies about the privacy protections they offer to customers. The EFF has continued to update results from the survey as companies have adjusted upward the protections they offer (see Figure 6-4). The EFF is particularly concerned with operational protocols and mechanical features that protect consumers' data in the event a government agency or other substantive body physically taps into the service's fiber-optic (or other) data lines. The focus of the EFF survey isn't mere paranoid hand-waving. The NSA was involved in just such line-tapping within the jurisdiction of its MUSCULAR program, affecting the data of millions of end users.

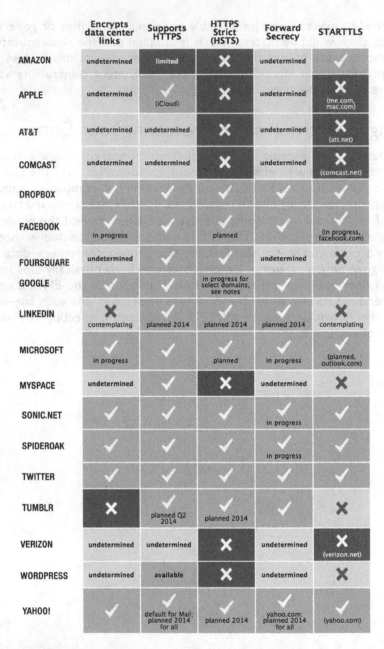

	Encrypts data center links	Supports HTTPS	HTTPS Strict (HSTS)	Forward Secrecy	STARTTLS
AMAZON	undetermined	limited	✗	undetermined	✓
APPLE	undetermined	✓ (iCloud)	✗	undetermined	✗ (me.com, mac.com)
AT&T	undetermined	undetermined	✗	undetermined	✗ (att.net)
COMCAST	undetermined	undetermined	✗	undetermined	✗ (comcast.net)
DROPBOX	✓	✓	✓	✓	✓
FACEBOOK	✓ in progress	✓	planned	✓	✓ (In progress, facebook.com)
FOURSQUARE	undetermined	✓	✓	undetermined	✗
GOOGLE	✓	✓	in progress for select domains, see notes	✓	✓
LINKEDIN	✗ contemplating	✓ planned 2014	✓ planned 2014	✓ planned 2014	✗ contemplating
MICROSOFT	✓ in progress	✓	planned	✓ in progress	✓ (planned, outlook.com)
MYSPACE	undetermined	✓	✗	undetermined	✗
SONIC.NET	✓	✓	✓	✓ in progress	✓
SPIDEROAK	✓	✓	✓	✓ in progress	✓
TWITTER	✓	✓	✓	✓	✓
TUMBLR	✗	✓ planned Q2 2014	✓ planned 2014	✓	✗
VERIZON	undetermined	undetermined	✗	undetermined	✗ (verizon.net)
WORDPRESS	undetermined	available	✗	undetermined	✗
YAHOO!	✓	✓ default for Mail; planned 2014 for all	✓ planned 2014	yahoo.com: planned 2014 for all	✓ (yahoo.com)

Figure 6-4. The results of the Electronic Frontier Foundation's "Crypto Survey," as of June 2014. (This figure is a derivative of "Encrypt the Web Report, Who's Doing What", by the Electronic Frontier Foundation, used under CC BY 3.0. https://www.eff.org/encrypt-the-web-report.)

The EFF survey asked data storage providers to respond to several questions regarding privacy. Does the provider flag all "authentication cookies," small files used to store credentials, as secure, thus providing them only over an encrypted connection? Does the provider encrypt web sites with hypertext transfer protocol secure (HTTPS) by default? (HTTPS is the secure version of the web standard HTTP protocol.) Requiring HTTPS forces users' connections to adopt an encrypted channel at all times. Does the provider incorporate HTTP Strict Transport Security (HSTS), a technology that forces a secure connection? When HTTP HSTS is used, it is more difficult for attackers to "spoof" a secure connection. In effect, the browser looks at the connection twice, in different ways, to ensure that it is encrypted. In the case of e-mail providers, is STARTTLS used? STARTTLS is a protocol that encrypts transmitted e-mails, but the transmission is secure only if *both* the systems from which the e-mail is sent and received use it. Does the provider use "forward secrecy" for its encryption keys? The forward secrecy protocol prevents a compromised key from being used to read past e-mail communications. Each key is good for only the current session, not past or future connections. As a body, this set of operational steps provides end users some level of e-mail privacy.

Critical also here is retention of users' search privacy. In 2005, Apple was the first to introduce a "Private Browsing" mode, which it incorporated into the Safari browser. This operational mode, which is sometimes crudely referred to as "porn mode," is designed specifically to not store any cookies, cached files, or other location identifiers on a computer's hard drive. Google's Chrome browser followed in 2008 with an "Incognito" mode, and Microsoft's Internet Explorer (see Figure 6-5) and Mozilla Firefox added their own similar camouflage functionality in 2009. The most popular mobile device browsers also have added this functionality. In theory, when these filtering modes are used during an Internet search, Internet activities leave no traces on the local computer.

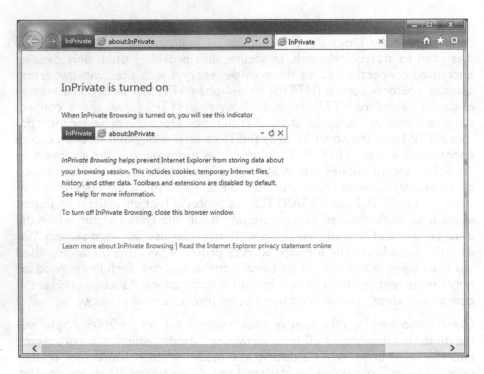

Figure 6-5. Microsoft calls the privacy mode in Internet Explorer InPrivate Browsing and presents this warning when it is activated. As of 2014, all major desktop and mobile browsers offer a similar feature

This works, in theory.... In practice, the various camouflage functions offered by Google, Microsoft, et. al are not 100 percent effective. These modes do effectively obscure searches stored on the local computer. However, a record of users' Internet activities can still be found on a corporate firewall, the telecom company's DNS (Domain Name Server [or System or Service]) equipment, or other network infrastructure. A more secure way to conceal Internet activities from prying eyes is through the use of a proxy browser.

A proxy browser can be used for additional privacy protection. A proxy browser, as the name implies, serves as a "proxy" for end users, disguising their true identity and location. The most well-known proxy browser, Tor, is a free tool that can be found easily on the Internet. Tor completely separates end users from their activities on the Internet. This does not mean that activities and users become invisible online. Rather, while a "snooping" government agency or corporation can identify the user, and can also identify sites that have been visited, snoops cannot connect the two sides of the equation and link users with sites. Tor obscures any connection between specific sites and specific users.

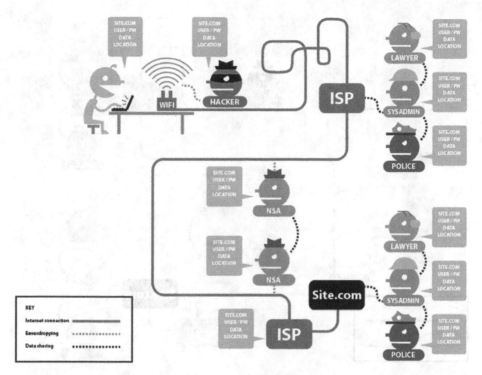

Figure 6-6. When using an insecure browser and the HTTP protocol, a user's complete set of activities, location, credentials, and other data are available to a hacker, a government agency monitoring the connection, the user's ISP, and any groups these agencies collaborate with

Tor actually uses an onion as its logo to advance the analogy of inserting "layers" between what a user does and the identification of those activities. Users' data and identity are protected as traffic is routed through several different Internet relays (see Figures 6-6 and 6-7). For example, when a non-proxy browser (such as Apple Safari or Google Chrome) is used to browse to a web site (such as cnn.com), that traffic passes from users' devices, to their ISP or telecom provider (Verizon, AT&T, Comcast, etc.), to CNN's servers, and back again. If no specific precautions are taken, users' identity, their physical location, and their desired web site (along with any related credentials) are totally visible to the destination site, the telecom provider, and any eavesdropping organizations that happen to be paying attention.

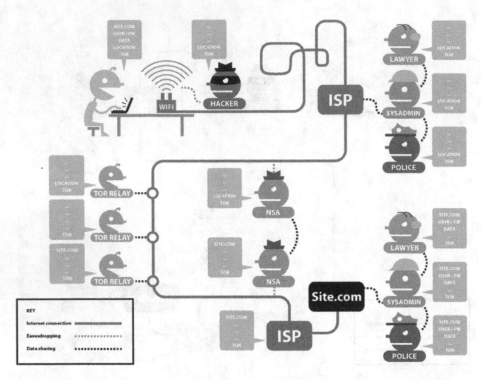

Figure 6-7. When using the Tor browser and the HTTPS protocol, the user's traffic is routed through a series of Tor "relays." A hacker, a government agency, and the user's ISP can see some of the user's data, but not all of it together. The site being visited gets most of the user's data, but not his or her specific location/identity, which is obscured by Tor. (Figures from the Electronic Frontier Foundation, used with permission under the terms of a Creative Commons license [http://creativecommons.org/licenses/by/3.0/us/].)

In contrast, when using a browser such as Tor, user traffic is bounced through several relays on the way both to and from the destination. Each Internet relay has access to only one layer. Tor is often used to circumvent filters that organizations impose to block social media, news sites, and other potential "time wasters" that can distract employees during work hours. Because Tor systematically obscures the source of online traffic through this relayed approach, content filters cannot identify prohibited web sites or other sources and correctly block them.

Somewhat ominously, it appears that the NSA is focusing more attention specifically on Tor users. Code for an NSA program called XKeyscore has been analyzed by researchers. The software seems to focus specific surveillance activity on users outside the United States who visit the Tor home page or even conduct Internet searches for private browsing options.[9] Ironically, for users concerned about their online privacy the best defense may be a good offense. The larger the Tor user base grows, the harder it will be for governments to track individual Tor users, who increasingly become, in essence, a user block.

Private searching isn't easily done without switching to a separate browser. However, another approach to conceal or protect Internet searches is to use a search engine called DuckDuckGo (DDG). DuckDuckGo does not store IP addresses or user information. In August 2010 DDG announced a collaboration with the Tor network allowing for completely anonymous end-to-end Internet searches. DuckDuckGo may be developing into a more serious competitor for established search engines like Google and Bing. Users can "switch" to DuckDuckGo simply by opening duckduckgo.com in their web browser, instead of google.com or bing.com. DDG is poised to get even easier to use in the near future. In June of 2014 Apple announced that DuckDuckGo will be an available search option in the Safari browser in the upcoming versions of both its desktop (OS X 10.10) and mobile (iOS 8) operating systems.

Data at Rest

Different possibilities emerge when the issue is the protection of users' "local" data. This kind of in situ protection begins with whole disk encryption (WDE). Modern operating systems available through Apple and Microsoft include options offering users the capability to encrypt their entire hard drive. This means that, without a proper password or other authentication method, any data stored on the hard drive are inaccessible. For example, if a thief steals a laptop incorporating an encrypted hard drive, he or she can't access the drive without knowing the encryption password. Even if the thief physically removes the hard drive from the laptop, the contents will be scrambled gibberish. Apple calls its WDE variant FileVault. Microsoft refers to its product as BitLocker. There also are third-party offerings on the market, which include commercial products like Symantec's PGP Whole Disk Encryption and Sophos SafeGuard and the open source DiskCryptor.

Application of the WDE process provides users with reasonable assurance (against the casual or commercial snoop) that only authorized users can gain access to their computer. Most systems incorporate a PIN or password authentication gate. Other systems use a smart card or token in lieu of (or increasingly in conjunction with) a password in multilevel protection schemes.

---

[9] Ars Technia, Cyrus Farivar, "Report: Rare Leaked NSA Source Code Reveals Tor Servers Targeted," http://arstechnica.com/tech-policy/2014/07/report-rare-leaked-nsa-source-code-reveals-tor-servers-targeted/, July 3, 2014.

Without access to the proper logon credentials or materials, all of the data stored on the hard drive remain encrypted and unreadable. The end user of course may be forced or coerced into providing logon credentials, through threat of legal action or physical violence. The latter is referred to as "rubber-hose cryptanalysis"—mitigating the protection offered through WDE.

Previously, we hedged, noting that WDE offers reasonable assurance of protection against unauthorized computer access. In reality, it is possible that even the most sophisticated WDE may not protect against government surveillance. In September 2013, the *New York Times* reported that the NSA had circumvented or cracked most corporate and consumer encryption tools. Some of these private systems had been accessed through stealth approaches. In other cases, surprisingly, manufacturers had actually collaborated in this effort and inserted a "back door" at the government's request, allowing unfettered systems access.[10]

In light of evidence pointing to the widespread erosion of protocols protecting individual privacy, until recently a popular alternative to corporate WDE products, and one believed to be independent of NSA surveillance, was a product called TrueCrypt. Released in 2004, TrueCrypt was an open source product, developed for noncommercial use and available for free download. In true techno-thriller fashion, the product was developed by an anonymous group known only as the "TrueCrypt Foundation." The software was multiplatform, supporting Windows, Mac, and Linux PCs. Surprisingly, given its obscure parentage, many organizations recommended TrueCrypt as an officially sanctioned encryption product. Its multiplatform capability, corporate independence, ease of use, and the fact that it was free (!) likely off-set the mystery of its origins, making it enormously attractive.

In an effort to confirm the security offered by TrueCrypt, an audit of the software was successfully crowd-funded in October 2013. Continuing the techno-thriller theme, a group calling itself the "Open Crypto Audit Project" claimed to be in contact with the anonymous developers, who announced their support of the project. The first phase of the audit, completed in April 2014, reported finding no significant vulnerabilities in the software and no evidence of "back doors." The second and final phase of the audit was scheduled for completion in October 2014. In the interim, on May 28, 2014, TrueCrypt's developers announced that the project would be discontinued. A new version of the software was released that could decrypt files but that could not encrypt them. Speculation among security professionals focused on whether

---

[10]*New York Times*, Nicole Perlroth, Jeff Larson, and Scott Shane, "N.S.A. Able to Foil Basic Safeguards of Privacy on Web," www.nytimes.com/2013/09/06/us/nsa-foils-much-internet-encryption.html?ref=us, September 5, 2013.

TrueCrypt had been forced to cease operations by a government agency, or whether the software had somehow been exploited or compromised. As of the writing of this book, no evidence of a security compromise had been unearthed. Further thickening the plot, there has been no recorded occurrence of TrueCrypt encryption having been "cracked," or data being obtained from an encrypted machine without the password.

■ **Note**   As an extended aside, US courts have generally ruled that a private citizen cannot be forced to divulge an encryption password. This is considered "self-incrimination" and a violation of the protections offered by the Fifth Amendment.

Additional Reading

For more on protecting your data from eavesdroppers, see the following links, and visit our web site at www.10donts.com/snoops.

- *Wired* magazine's "Threat Level" blog, which focuses on issues of online privacy, security, and crime: www.wired. com/category/threatlevel/

- The Electronic Frontier Foundation's "EFF's Encrypt the Web Report," tracking the major Internet companies and their levels of data privacy: www.eff.org/encrypt-the-web-report

- Gizmodo, "Tor Is for Everyone: Why You Should Use Tor," featuring an explanation of Tor's features and a walkthrough on how to use it: http://gizmodo.com/tor-is-for-everyone-why-you-should-use-tor-1591191905

- Lifehacker, "How to Encrypt Your Email and Keep Your Conversations Private," featuring a detailed guide on using PGP for e-mail encryption: http://lifehacker. com/how-to-encrypt-your-email-and-keep-your-conversations-p-1133495744

- *Daily Mail*, "The Edward Snowden Guide to Encryption," with screenshots and the full video produced by Snowden: www.dailymail.co.uk/news/article-2628082/The-Edward-Snowden-guide-encryption-Fugitives-12-minute-homemade-video-ahead-leaks-explaining-avoid-NSA-tracking-emails.html

- *PC World*, "Three Practical Reasons to Use Your Browser's Private Mode," with explanations and instructions: www. pcworld.com/article/2106766/three-practical-reasons-to-use-your-browsers-private-mode.html

- *PC World*, "So Long, TrueCrypt: 5 Alternative Encryption Tools That Can Lock Down Your Data," with reviews and links to built-in OS encryption methods and third-party options: www.pcworld.com/article/2304851/so-long-truecrypt-5-encryption-alternatives-that-can-lock-down-your-data.html

Don't Be Careless with Your Phone

We're Going Mobile...

Jason is the regional manager of a large restaurant franchise, overseeing operations for 32 limited-menu restaurants in a major metropolitan area in the Northwest. Although his work requires him to be in regular daily contact with his location mangers and suppliers, his corporate parent does not provide him with a corporate cell phone. Jason uses his own phone in a bring your own device (BYOD) arrangement to send and receive e-mail from his corporate account and communicate with his managers and assistant managers as well as his supply chain contacts. In order to connect to his company's e-mail server, Jason is required to use a four-digit PIN on his phone. Some other rules and regulations are displayed on screen, but Jason simply clicks "agree" without reading those.

While on a rare vacation, Jason's phone is stolen. He uses his wife's phone to call his IT department about changing his e-mail password. IT informs him that because the phone was connected to the company's servers, IT can remotely erase the phone—even though it is a personally owned device! Jason is a bit unnerved by this level of control, but the IT rep reminds him that he agreed to this policy when he connected his phone to the corporate e-mail server. In this case, this level of corporate control is useful, as Jason's personal and work-related data are remotely wiped from the phone, eliminating any chance of data or identity theft related to the loss of his device at the beach.

Mobility in the 21st Century

Although broadly a discussion of mobile devices, here we focus primarily on smartphones because they've become almost an appendage in modern society. In the information age we're living in, men, women, and children of all ages—all of us—have our phones with us nearly everywhere we go, at nearly every minute of the day, irrespective of social setting (playground with our kids, public bathroom, restaurant, airplane, waiting room at the doctor's office, etc.). We also use the word "phone" somewhat euphemistically, as this designation is unquestionably a gross misnomer. These devices have become so powerful and perform so many other functions that often, really, the "phone" portion of the device is among its least relevant attributes.

In a full actualization of the current possibilities offered through these powerful tools, we have become truly mobile as a society. Most everyone you know, and most everyone they know, is connected virtually. For example, the Pew Research Center recently reported that 90 percent of Americans now own at least one cell phone, and 58 percent own a smartphone.[1] We're not only passively connected through these devices, we're also seeking connections. For example, a related study finds that 67 percent of cell phone users frequently check their devices for new messages, even when there's been no alert tone or signal indicating contact has been attempted. This desire for connectivity doesn't extend merely to the daylight hours when we're conscious; 44 percent of respondents reported that they sleep with their phone at their bedside, to make sure that they don't miss any calls, text messages, or other communications during the night! In every conventional sense we are essentially tethered to our mobile devices nearly all of the time. This functional indivisibility also increases our vulnerability to potential threats orbiting these omnipresent devices, which should create strong incentives to increase our caution and vigilance.

In what is an odd quirk of standard operating procedure in the 21st century, it can be by no means taken for granted that employees will use company-owned machines to do their work. The fuzzy divide between work accomplished on personal vs. corporate-owned equipment is reflected in the dual philosophies of bring your own device and corporate-owned, personally enabled (COPE) devices.

When It's the Employee's Device, but the Company's Resources—BYOD

Many companies around the world equip employees with cell phones and require perpetual reachability and communication as a quasi-formal aspect

---

[1]Pew Research Internet Project, "Mobile Technology Fact Sheet," www.pewinternet.org/fact-sheets/mobile-technology-fact-sheet/, January 2014.

of the employment contract. At companies not provisioning a mobile device and/or service, many employees use their own personal equipment to perform work-related tasks, bringing these to the office and connecting them to organizational networks and other resources.

This practice has come to be known as BYOD, or bring your own device, and it is growing. A recent global survey of CIOs reported by Gartner, Inc., finds that 38 percent of companies plan to stop providing employees with mobile devices by 2016.[2] Although the device may be owned by an employee, when personal devices connect to company networks or digital resources, company policies govern their use and can directly affect individuals' autonomy vis a vis the device itself. As with Jason the restaurant executive, when connecting to corporate e-mail servers, users often give IT staff the right to track, lock, and even remotely erase their cell phone in the event of loss or theft. The device and service technically belong to the employee, who keeps the device even in the event of turnover. Employees also decide when they want to upgrade their hardware, modify their service levels, or change their phone number, etc., because the phone is their private property.

When It's the Company's Device, but Used at the Employee's Discretion—COPE

Although some employees carry two cell phones to work—one assigned by their company and one personal—many professionals don't want to carry around two mobile devices if it is possible to avoid this unwieldy arrangement. As an alternative both to the cumbersome two-device model and BYOD, organizations are increasingly adopting an approach known as COPE, which stands for corporate-owned, personally enabled.[3] What this means is that although the device is technically owned by the organization, it is not "locked down" to work-only functionality. Employees to whom COPE devices are assigned can use them for personal business, receive and make personal calls, send and receive personal e-mails and text messages, install apps, surf the Web, take photos, watch movies, and listen to music, in addition to all of the other functions that a modern smartphone can perform.

---

[2] Gartner, "Gartner Predicts by 2017, Half of Employers Will Require Employees to Supply Their Own Device for Work Purposes," www.gartner.com/newsroom/id/2466615, May 1, 2013.
[3] *Financial Post*, Lynn Greiner, "Beyond BYOD: Welcome to the Era of COPE (Corporate Owned, Personally Enabled) Devices," http://business.financialpost.com/2014/02/03/beyond-byod-welcome-to-the-era-of-cope-corporate-owned-personally-enabled-devices/?__lsa=5553-a83a, February 3, 2014.

Although much more loosely constrained than strictly work-tied equipment, the uses to which employees can put COPE phones may not be completely unfettered. Users are still likely to be required to comply with corporate policies regarding the use of a PIN, pornography downloads, and explicit messages, for example. Of course, because the device isn't personal property, an employee must leave it behind if he or she leaves the organization.

Assignment or reassignment of the device is at the discretion of the company, as is the phone number and decisions about upgrades or changes in service levels, including, for example, monthly call/text/data allowances, because it is a company-owned resource. Employees' convenience is enhanced—they have only one device, and IT handles any device issues—but autonomy with regard to use is essentially gone. Under both the BYOD and COPE models, it is essential that employees understand their rights and responsibilities pertaining to their mobile devices.

Know Your Rights

What happens if the device is lost or stolen? How and to whom should this issue be reported, and what are the next steps following the loss? What are the usage parameters associated with the device? What is and, perhaps more important, what is not allowed with respect to using the device? If the device is corporate-owned, what are the monthly limits on data, calls, texts, and other media? Is it permissible to use the device for personal communication and business? Is it permissible to let someone else (children, spouse, etc.) use the device and to know the PIN or password? Is using the device on non-corporate wireless networks, while at home or during travel, permitted? In our chapter opener, Jason did the right things by reporting the loss of his phone to IT personnel at his company and changing his password. While he was surprised that the IT department was able to remotely erase his phone, he almost certainly agreed to this policy when he first connected this device to his company's e-mail server.

Knowing the answers to these questions can help individuals avoid putting themselves in breach of explicit (yet perhaps unrecognized) operational agreements, putting their personal or work-related data at risk, and unceremoniously losing their job.

Physically Securing Your Phone

As we've sought to highlight throughout earlier chapters in this book, modern smartphone users store a wide variety of critical data on these powerful devices. A majority of Americans and users throughout the world have come to recognize this as a critical operational fact in their personal and professional lives. An emerging implication of the phones' massive storage capacity and increasing commoditization is that loss of the data stored on the device often can be substantially more financially injurious than loss of the device itself. In light of this potentially massive vulnerability, all smartphone users should systematically perform several basic steps to protect themselves and their data. These steps bear directly on the delicate balance between ease and security, simultaneously increasing data security and decreasing ease-of-use.

Start Me Up—but Not Without a Password

First, as a foundational point of departure always—*always*—use a startup PIN, password, or fingerprint key, every time you unlock the phone. Yes, this step adds several seconds to the process of accessing the device. But, absent this most basic protective step, a thief can very easily access every bit of data stored on the device, and a substantial proportion of users' web-based identity data as well. This step has simply become a sine qua non for mobile device safety in the 21st century. This is less a seat-belt issue than an engine issue. Commonly, mobile devices are used to store passwords for e-mail accounts, social media such as Facebook, and web stores such as Amazon, among other Internet-based services and activities. Most banking and credit card sites and apps will not allow for stored passwords, but some do. A locked gate is the bare minimum protocol that users should follow to protect their smartphones. Every smartphone user should have a PIN on his or her device that is at least four digits in length. Even though this is an absolutely foundational requirement to avoid potentially catastrophic losses, a 2014 *Consumer Reports* study finds that only 54 percent of Americans use any type of PIN or password protection on their phones![4]

This astonishing nonchalance is all the more frightening in light of the finding, from the same study, that in 2013 3.1 million phones were stolen in the United States alone. Although hard to fathom in a world where identity theft costs Americans more than $1.5 billion annually,[5] extrapolating from these *Consumer Reports* data, nearly 1.5 million of the smartphones that were stolen had no protection whatsoever! Android, iOS, and Windows phones provide users with both simple (4-digit numeric) and more complex (longer, possibly alphanumeric) pass-code options. Whenever it is feasible to do so, users should choose more complex password options for the added security they

---

[4]*Consumer Reports*, "Smart Phone Thefts Rose to 3.1 Million Last Year, *Consumer Reports* Finds," www.consumerreports.org/cro/news/2014/04/smart-phone-thefts-rose-to-3-1-million-last-year/index.htm, May 28, 2014.
[5]*Huffington Post*, "Identity Theft Cost Americans $1.52 Billion in 2011, FTC Says," www.huffingtonpost.com/2012/02/28/identity-theft-cost-americans-152-billion-2011-ftc_n_1307485.html, February 28, 2012.

offer. A thief or visual trespasser looking over a user's shoulder can fairly easily identify the number buttons pressed in any given four-digit sequence. With longer codes that incorporate the entire keyboard, numbers and letters, this sort of "shoulder surfing" is much more difficult.

When setting up a password for your phone, use common sense, just as with any other password you use to protect your other devices. Don't use your name, your birth date, your address, your spouse's name, or any publicly available information that can be linked directly to you. Don't give your PIN or password to anyone else. If someone needs to borrow your phone for any reason, enter the password yourself before handing it over. If your kids use any of your protected devices, don't let them share your password with their friends. Teach them not to yell across a crowded room, "Hey, Dad, is your iPhone password still "8675309?" Although we are creatures of habit who don't do particularly well with any kind of change, don't be afraid to change your PIN/password, particularly if you have reason to suspect that someone else has learned it. Is this just common sense? It's hard to tell given that millions of users fail to adopt even the most rudimentary level of protection.

When a Password Isn't Enough

Some phone manufacturers have begun to offer users alternatives to conventional passwords that may effectively increase the incidence of user self-protection. Apple's iPhone 5S and HTC's One Max (both released in 2013) were the first smartphones to offer fingerprint recognition in lieu of a password or PIN. Android smartphones running version 4.1 of the operating system (code named "Jelly Bean") or later can use the "face unlock" feature. With this techno-thriller-esque innovation, a facial recognition protocol can substitute for a pass-code login. Users of these devices also can use "pattern unlock" by swiping their fingers on the screen in a preset, user-selected pattern. However, some security experts have warned that over time smudges on the screen have the potential to reveal the correct unlock pattern, diminishing the utility of this method for maintaining device security.

The data stored on unlocked phones are also vulnerable if the device is stolen. In order to off-set this vulnerability users should set their phone to "lock" itself, thus requiring the re-entry of a pass-code after a fairly short idle period of no more than five minutes. Smartphone operating system settings also can be used to restrict the type of data that can be displayed on the lock screen absent a correct pass-code. For example, by default, both Android and iOS devices will display incoming text messages on the lock screen, which of course represents a security issue if the device has been stolen. Users also can choose an option that erases the data stored on their phone after a specified number of incorrect password attempts—commonly 10, but a smaller number can be chosen.

Losing (and Finding!) the Key to Your Digital Life

Missing phones also aren't necessarily gone for good. Users can enable a setting on a phone that allows it to be physically tracked and located if it is lost or stolen. Apple calls its version of this recovery service Find My iPhone; on Android phones it's referred to as Android Device Manager, and Microsoft's tool is called Find My Phone (see Figure 7-1). While the provider-specific features and user protocols associated with this tool vary (see links at the end of this chapter), each system allows users to locate their device on a map, lock it with a PIN, make it ring, play an alarm, display a message, and remotely erase the device. All of these functionalities are likely to be both off-putting to a thief and informative to an honest person who happens to come across a lost phone.

Find My Phone

Windows Phone	Phone location	Ring
NOKIA Nokia Lumia	New York, NY	Lock
ICON	3/11/2014 11:01 AM	Erase
	Refresh | Print | Center on map	

Figure 7-1. *Microsoft's Find My Phone feature (and similar features on Android and iOS devices) allows end users to locate a missing phone on a map or make it ring (if lost) and lock or erase the phone (if stolen)*

Of course, these functions work only if the device is turned on and is connected to a cellular or wireless network. When using a corporate-owned device or a personally owned device that connects to organizational networks, some of these policies will be set a priori by corporate IT. For example, when using a Microsoft Exchange server (the most commonly used corporate e-mail system in the United States), mobile devices connect using a protocol called "ActiveSync." ActiveSync makes options available to system administrators about policies, which are enforced on mobile phones before users are allowed to connect to the server. These policies can include use of a PIN or pass-code with a pre-established level of required complexity, a number of "bad password" attempts allowed before an automatic erase of the device, the ability to track the physical location of the device, and the ability to remotely erase the device à la "Jason" from our chapter introduction. Whether users operate a BYOD or COPE device, it is critical that they read the "fine print" when connecting to corporate systems and know their rights as well as constraints on the parameters of their of use.

Mobile Law

As we've highlighted in earlier chapters, users' data are frequently subjected to scrutiny by both commercial and governmental agents focused on usage patterns and social connections. Snoops of various flavors go to great lengths to circumvent steps users take to maintain their privacy and identity on the Internet. These intrusive entities are focused not only on activities originating from computers and laptops, but also on mobile activities. Given the preponderance of web-based activity conducted from mobile vs. in situ technology, it is important that in June 2014, the Supreme Court unanimously ruled that cell phones are protected from warrantless searches. In issuing a ruling resolving two cases (*Riley v. California* and *United States v. Wurie*), the Court stated that police searches of cell phones without a warrant represented a violation of the Fourth Amendment's protection against unreasonable search and seizure. Chief Justice John Roberts wrote for the Court: "The fact that technology now allows an individual to carry such information in his hand does not make the information any less worthy of the protection for which the Founders fought."[6]

---

[6]CNET, Ben Fox Rubin, "Supreme Court: Cell Phones Are Protected from Warrantless Searches," www.cnet.com/news/supreme-court-cell-phones-protected-from-warrantless-searches/, June 25, 2014.

Insecure Background Wireless Networks

In Chapter 5, we addressed a range of issues concerning the use of wireless networks on the road in coffee shops, hotels, airports, public toilets, etc. This discussion was focused primarily on intentional wireless network access where, for example, a user sits down in a convention center to check e-mail or logs in to the Wi-Fi available at a coffee shop. The intentional accessing of unveiled Wi-Fi represents one kind of danger. The powerful mobile technologies available today, however, expose users to an entirely different kind of danger when phones connect to wireless networks without either users' consent or knowledge.

Don't Trust a Wireless Network Based on Its Name

In June 2014 NPR produced a segment for the "All Tech Considered" program, in conjunction with the tech news site Ars Technica[7] that reported, "There is a hole in mobile security that could make tens of millions of Americans vulnerable." With Xfinitywifi, Comcast is rolling out what it hopes will become a nationwide wireless network for subscribers that piggy-backs the Wi-Fi of private users. AT&T is engaged in a similar effort, offering free Wi-Fi at over 11,000 McDonald's locations in the United States[8] as well as many other restaurants, airports, hotel lobbies, and other public locations. Providers including Google and Sprint are seeking to develop like infrastructure, but Comcast and AT&T are currently the two biggest players in this space. These two networks each use a common name, a nationwide name. Comcast's framework is called Xfinity WiFi, while AT&T calls its architecture AT&T Wi-Fi.

The first time users connect to either one of these two networks, they have to make an explicit choice to do so. In all subsequent future sessions, however, their mobile devices (by default) remember the names of previously used networks and reconnect whenever it is possible to do so. The dangers associated with this automatic reconnect are genuine. First, there is nothing stopping a criminal hacker from creating a wireless network with one of these two names. This artificial lure can easily trap users' whose devices are tricked into connecting with a counterfeit network. Even when the phone isn't being actively used, such as when it is stored in a pocket or purse, the

---

[7]NPR, Steve Henn, "Here's One Big Way Your Mobile Phone Could Be Open to Hackers," www.npr.org/blogs/alltechconsidered/2014/06/13/321389989/heres-one-big-way-your-mobile-phone-could-be-open-to-hackers, June 13, 2014.
[8]McDonald's, "Free Wi-Fi @ McDonald's," www.mcdonalds.com/us/en/services/free_wifi.html.

apps on the phone are transmitting and receiving data. Ars Technica reported that e-mail, social media, calendar, mapping, and other apps constantly exchange data with central servers.[9] An attacker can easily gather a great deal of information about users whose smartphones are connected to a rogue network, and this requires no intention or explicit interaction with users. Mobile devices and the networks to which they connect are communicating with one another while users are in absentia.

Don't Trust Your Phone to Connect for You

In April 2014, Microsoft announced the 8.1 release of its Windows Phone software for mobile devices. Included in the new features is a wireless auto-connecting option, which Microsoft calls "Wi-Fi Sense" (see Figure 7-2). Microsoft touts this feature as a way for consumers to save money, using Wi-Fi data where available in lieu of potentially more expensive cellular data.[10] Wi-Fi Sense connects users' devices to publicly available open networks, even automatically accepting the terms of use page for users, providing their name, phone number, and/or e-mail address as authentication to wireless hotspots that require these bona fides. While presumably wildly convenient and economical for frequent travelers, this protocol also represents a potentially enormous security risk. Again, the more a user's phone does automatically without explicit interaction or direction, the greater the risk to the user's data and identity.

---

[9]Ars Technica, Sean Gallagher, "Ars Tests Internet Surveillance—by Spying on an NPR Reporter," http://arstechnica.com/security/2014/06/what-the-nsa-or-anyone-can-learn-about-you-from-internet-traffic/, June 10, 2014.
[10]Windows Phone, "Use Wi-Fi Sense to Get Connected," www.windowsphone.com/en-us/how-to/wp8/connectivity/use-wi-fi-sense-to-get-connected.

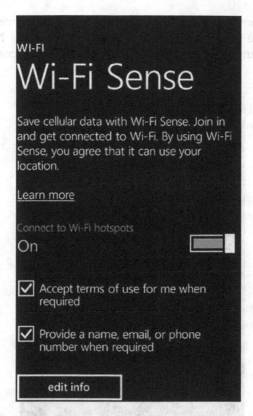

Figure 7-2. Microsoft's Wi-Fi Sense feature, added in Windows Phone 8.1, can provide personal data to available wireless networks without the user's direct instruction

So, how can users protect themselves against passive capture? First, turn off Wi-Fi on all devices when they're not in use. Again, although this step represents an obvious trade-off in the convenience-security balance, avoiding invisible seizure requires such concessions. Enter the Wi-Fi settings on your device and turn off the "auto-connect" option. Also delete any "one-off" Wi-Fi networks such as Xfinity WiFi or AT&T Wi-Fi if you don't plan to use them often (see Figure 7-3). It is important to remember that these nationwide networks are in their infancy—with the inherent liabilities of newness. In the future it is likely that these telecoms will find more effective ways to encrypt subscribers' data in transit. They also are likely to find better ways to ensure that devices aren't being tricked into joining rogue networks set up by criminals as an attractive lure. However, dampening this rosy speculation, the companies quoted by NPR were not particularly encouraging or forthcoming as to their steps in this direction. NPR quotes, "AT&T said it took extraordinary measures to keep its consumer safe. Comcast said it was planning to roll out a more secure Wi-Fi network sometime in the future. But it didn't say when."[11] Neither of these sentiments offers any substantive foundation to buoy user confidence.

Figure 7-3. Modern mobile devices remember the wireless networks to which they have been connected. Over time, this can build into a substantial list. It is a good practice periodically to "clean out" this list and remove wireless networks users don't plan to use again

Bluetooth Hacking

A relatively minor avenue of vulnerability for mobile phones, still worthy of attention, is through the now ubiquitous Bluetooth we see in offices, cars, and headsets. Bluetooth is a wireless protocol developed in the early 1990s for short-range communication between (or among) computers, tablets,

---

[11]NPR, "Here's One Big Way Your Mobile Phone Could Be Open to Hackers," www.npr.org/templates/transcript/transcript.php?storyId=321389989, June 13, 2014.

smartphones, and other devices. On the desktop it's commonly used for wireless keyboards and mice. In the car, it's the protocol that allows users to communicate hands-free using their cell phone. It also can be used for wireless headphones and headsets, in conjunction with a phone, tablet, or music player. Less common but still widespread, Bluetooth can be used for direct communication between two devices to transfer data. For this kind of data transfer the devices have to be physically proximal (typically within 30 feet), and both users have to agree to the connection. This short-range data transfer capacity can be dangerous for unsuspecting users.

To protect yourself against a Bluetooth hack, read the screens and dialog boxes that appear on your phone. Don't automatically click "Yes" or "OK" if a file transfer or other connection is requested. If you didn't initiate the transfer, don't agree to it! It also is important to turn Bluetooth off altogether if there is no immediate need for it to be on. Turning off the function carries with it the added advantage of increasing battery life on mobile devices. Or, if you do use Bluetooth for hands-free or other (non-file-transfer) purposes, turn off the "discoverable" option in your settings. This will make your phone invisible to other Bluetooth users and so take your device out of the pool hackers search for potential targets.

Malware Apps

Malware is software that is designed to achieve some malicious intent, that users did not intend to install and are likely unaware has been installed on their devices. Historically, malware infected users' computers. Not surprisingly, this threat is no longer limited to computers per se but is seeing increasing rates of infection on a wider range of platforms. Mobile malware is becoming much more common.

In June 2014, McAfee Labs reported that the spread of mobile malware had increased by 167 percent over the levels observed in the previous year.[12] This is not an accident. Malware developers often take advantage of the popularity of other apps and try to emulate them to entice users to download their programs. For example, the McAfee report found that there were numerous active clones of the popular game Flappy Bird (an app removed from the market in February 2014), and that 79 percent of these clones contained some variant of malware code. Malware also disproportionately appears on the Android platform; 97 percent of mobile malware is found on Android apps.

---

[12]*Forbes*, Kate Vinton, "Mobile Malware Is on the Rise, McAfee Report Reveals," www.forbes.com/sites/katevinton/2014/06/24/mobile-malware-is-on-the-rise-mcafee-report-reveals/, June 24, 2014.

The vast majority of this software comes from third-party app stores, not the official Google Play Store.[13] As a consequence, at this moment, avoiding these mobile traps can be accomplished in a fairly straightforward way. Android users should simply download all of their apps through Google Play, as apps distributed through this venue are subjected to rigorous testing and screening. For example, the security firm F-Secure found that only 0.1 percent of the apps available at the official Play Store were malware-infected, and those were quickly removed from Google Play inventory.

But, the Google Play Store is not available worldwide. As a consequence, users in other countries (primarily in Asia and the Middle East) are forced to use third-party app stores, some of which do not screen their apps as well as Google. For an additional layer of security against the threat of mobile malware, Android users should download and run a mobile anti-malware app. Some options for effective prophylaxis include Antivirus Security Free, produced by AVG, and Norton Security Antivirus, offered by Symantec, which can protect against a wide range of potential mobile malware threats. Both the Apple and Microsoft app stores, which employ similar screening rules and policies to those used by Google Play, were found to be free of malware apps.

Operating System Updates

We discuss the importance of keeping all of your operating systems updated in Chapter 8. Here, it is important to remember that mobile devices today also rely on an operating system infrastructure. Although we often think of them by default in a static way, these devices really are more "computer" than "phone." While conventional phones (imagine a rotary dial and big, black, clunky handset mounted to the wall with a long twisted curly wire...) don't require updating, computers do. As the nature of the threats to which your mobile devices are exposed continues to evolve, the gates behind which you can effectively protect them depend on updating as well. It is critical to keep all of your mobile devices current with operating system updates, security patches, and other essential software downloads regularly offered by hardware and software manufacturers.

---

[13]*Forbes*, Gordon Kelly, "Report: 97% of Mobile Malware Is on Android. This Is the Easy Way You Stay Safe," www.forbes.com/sites/gordonkelly/2014/03/24/report-97-of-mobile-malware-is-on-android-this-is-the-easy-way-you-stay-safe/, March 24, 2014.

Additional Reading

For more on protecting your data from eavesdroppers, see the following links and visit our web site at www.10donts.com/mobile:

- CNET, "Essential Steps for Securing Your Phone, and What Else Can Be Done to Foil Thieves," a great resource with step-by-step guidelines for securing iOS, Android, and Microsoft devices: www.cnet.com/how-to/essential-steps-for-securing-your-phone-and-what-else-can-be-done-to-foil-thieves/

- Yahoo! Tech, "How to Track and Secure Your Lost or Stolen Phone, No Matter Who Made It," a helpful overall guide to smartphone security: www.yahoo.com/tech/how-to-track-and-secure-your-lost-or-stolen-phone-no-83728804256.html

- Wired, "Companies Weigh BYOD vs. COPE, but What Really Protects Data?" a look at the risks inherent in both approaches: www.wired.com/2013/05/companies-weigh-byod-vs-cope-but-what-really-protects-data/

- Privacy Rights Clearinghouse, "Bring Your Own Device... at Your Own Risk," a look at employee liabilities when using BYOD in the workplace: www.privacyrights.org/bring-your-own-device-risks

- Android Authority, "14 Best Antivirus Android Apps and Anti-Malware Android Apps," with detailed reviews: www.androidauthority.com/10-best-antivirus-apps-for-android-269696/

Don't Use Dinosaurs

They're Extinct for a Reason

Sue is an experienced marketing vice president at a Fortune 100 athletics gear merchandising firm with a nationwide distribution and retailing network. She left her laptop at home while on vacation with her family, visiting her parents in the mountains, and didn't realize it was gone until she arrived. Sue feels naked without her computer. She also doesn't like to use other people's machines for her work. However, she had a few remaining things to get off her plate before she could really relax.

Her parents' machine runs an old version of Microsoft Office (2007), has out-of-date antivirus protection, and is generally ill-equipped to effectively fend off any concerted "modern" attack; nonetheless, Sue used the old XP desktop to check her work e-mail, revise some work-related documents, and update the parameters of several ongoing provider contracts. In all, Sue spent no more than a few hours working on the machine, but it required that she connect to the company server and several sensitive databases. She crossed her fingers, and typed fast, hoping that no one up in the mountains was looking to hack her connection. She got everything done quickly and, for the rest of the much-needed long weekend with her family, was able to put work out of her mind.

Several weeks later, Sue found out that her parents' computer contained several forms of malware and that as a consequence, both her work credentials and several company databases may have been compromised. Following mandated protocol, Sue immediately contacted her IT director when she found out, changed all of her passwords, and locked down all of the accounts she supervises, but tremors of concern resounded throughout her office. This sort of breach could easily represent a major financial loss to her company in the form of forfeited revenues, compromised confidential information, loss of customer data, malware-related downtime, public relations setbacks, and more.

Software: It Has an Expiration Date

As we've established at multiple points throughout our discussion thus far, the always-on nature of the modern Internet is both a blessing and a curse to users enmeshed in its limitless possibilities and engrossed, emboldened, empowered, and enthralled by its endless capabilities. On the one hand, it is a truly wonderful thing to have the power to sit down at a computer and almost instantaneously look up sports scores, make reservations, buy tickets, dash off an e-mail, get a weather report, check movie times, talk to a friend, read a book, and buy a shirt, plane tickets, or anything else that Amazon or myriad vendors sell. We all well remember the not-too-distant past when we had to dial up to connect to the Internet and the screeching noises of the modem and the 30–60 second delay necessary to get connected. No one wants to return to the cumbersome, time-consuming bad old days. But the always-on Internet also comes with real risks to both our data and our identity.

This risk emerges from the fact that, as long as our computers and other devices are connected to the Internet, the potential is there that they can be found and compromised by thieves looking to steal everything important stored in our machines. In order to protect against this literally ever-present threat, it is critical that users today keep up-to-date the software architecture that allows these constantly aging devices to function "safely" in this information-porous environment. This wasn't always so.

The "Good Old Days" of Software

Fifteen years ago, it didn't really matter if a user's home computer was still running the Windows 95 operating system four or five years after its first release. The "old" OS still ran most current software, and the functionality users experienced wasn't substantially different than they enjoyed with its immediate successor, Windows 98. In fact, most users with conventional computing needs wouldn't even notice. Users commonly kept their desktop computers (few had laptops) for six, eight, or even ten years, running the originally installed operating system and applications. Viruses, though they existed, were primitive and were generally propagated via floppy disks, not e-mail or the Internet. Applications like Microsoft Word weren't generally exploitable, so updating them was not critical.

However, the pace of technological innovation has continued to advance in an essentially exponential way. With the ever-increasing sophistication of criminals seeking to breach system security, extended operating system utility and safety is a thing of the past. The shelf-life of current operating systems and a great deal of productivity software as well has shortened directly in conjunction with increased speed, capacity, functionality, and criminal viciousness. Today, an outdated operating system, particularly one that is no longer receiving manufacturer security patches, represents an extreme liability for anyone using that machine for modern, connected computing.

New Software for a New Era

As highlighted in our previous discussion, hackers are always developing more sophisticated malware variants along a wider and wider range of attack vectors. They are as a category relentless and primarily profit driven, and they do not sleep. This has led to a virtual arms race, where each side is constantly challenged to take the next offensive step in battles with shifting, complex, dynamic lines of encounter. When criminals come up with a new vehicle for attacking the most up-to-date security systems, software developers create new defenses, the attackers find ways around these defenses, and the cycle continues—until it stops. When this happens, when the build-up becomes one sided, the nature of the cycle changes in a fundamental way.

When a manufacturer stops producing new updates for an operating system, when the software developers are no longer defending the battle lines, attackers have free rein to exploit all of the vulnerabilities that they can find in that system. What's more, because of the nature of modern information flow and unfettered, broad-scale dissemination, these vulnerabilities are publicized in an essentially viral way so other attackers can take advantage of them as well. Because gaps in the system's security are no longer being filled with protective software previously offered by manufacturers, until users adopt the next iteration of their device's operating system, criminals can gorge themselves on what they find on users' machines.

Don't Forget About Mobile Apps

As with computers 15 years ago, cell phones in the 1990s—even the first "smartphones" or PDA/phone combinations in the late 1990s and the early 2000s—were generally not upgradeable to more sophisticated operating platforms. Or, if these devices could be modified, upgrading them was an extremely tedious and complex process requiring that the phone be hard-connected to a computer. Wireless or "over-the-air" updates that are entirely taken for granted today were simply unheard of at the time—pure fantasy.

But, avoiding this cumbersome upgrading process didn't have any substantive impact on the safety of users' data or system security because hackers weren't pursuing mobile devices as a point of attack at this time. These devices also were not constantly connected to the Internet, so it was nearly impossible for an attacker to gain unauthorized access. Because these devices didn't use "apps" other than the preloaded stock functions that came on the phone from the factory, piggyback attacks also were not an option for cyber criminals. To a great extent, during this period mobile devices were all but immune from attack. However, this sepia-toned mobile exemption began to evaporate as the sophistication of modern devices increased their vulnerability. Modern smartphones are so powerful and also so Internet-connected that they have become for all intents and purposes minicomputers. In fact, many people increasingly use their smartphones for just this purpose in lieu of a traditional computer.[1] By extension, this also means that they have inherited some of the same kinds of risks (and benefits) as modern users of computers, tablets, and other "computing" devices. These risks can be great. Unquestionably, the broadest user-segment vulnerability today is found among users of the Windows XP operating system.

Windows XP

Windows XP, the fantastically successful operating system first released by Microsoft in 2001 and sold until 2010, is the best-selling operating system in history. Unofficial estimates place sales at nearly 1 billion copies.[2] However, in April 2014, support for the system was officially discontinued. Microsoft announced that it would produce no more security updates or patches for Windows XP. The cycle had come to an end.

In May 2014, Microsoft made a "single" exception to this official withdrawal and patched an exposed exploit to its Internet Explorer web browser. The software giant made this patch available for Windows XP despite official warnings. The Microsoft PR apparatus announced that this step was taken due to the exploit's "proximity to the end of support for Windows XP." Peter Bright, a regular contributor to the tech site Ars Technica, criticized Microsoft for this backpedal, writing "if Microsoft can blink once, who's to say it won't do so

---

[1] NJ.com, Allan Hoffman, "Seven Ways to Use Smartphone like a PC," www.nj.com/business/index.ssf/2013/01/hoffman_why_lug_a_laptop_when.html, January 18, 2013.
[2] ExtremeTech, Sebastian Anthony, "Windows XP Finally Put to Sleep by Microsoft—but It Will Still Haunt Us for Years to Come," www.extremetech.com/computing/180062-windows-xp-finally-put-to-sleep-by-microsoft-but-it-will-still-haunt-us-for-years-to-come, April 8, 2014.

again?"[3] Since making this one last patch publicly available, as of the writing of this book in July 2014, Microsoft had not yet "blinked" again. No further XP updates or security patches have since been released to the public. Perhaps Microsoft is really done with XP—time will tell.

The end of the XP era is quite ominous from a data security standpoint. As of April 2014 the market share owned by Windows XP was estimated to be hovering at just under a third of the entire market, with 28 percent of all Internet-connected computers utilizing the operating system. However, the actual percentage may be much higher, as significant numbers of XP machines are likely protected behind firewalls or not always connected to the Internet. This problem is not limited to users in the United States. For example, it is currently estimated that in China alone 50 percent of all desktop computers are still running Windows XP.[4] The scale of the problem is truly enormous. As of April 2014, an estimated 300 million computers worldwide were still running the depreciated XP operating system.[5] As we saw in the chapter opener, users like "Sue" may sometimes stumble across an older Windows XP computer while traveling or when in protracted transit and faced with lost baggage or other conventional setbacks (e.g., dead battery, no Wi-Fi).

Microsoft made a concerted public-relations effort in the several months leading up to the XP end date to communicate the impending vulnerability to users. This effort was intended to encourage private consumers, small businesses, and organizations with enterprise-level systems to upgrade or replace their XP computers altogether (see Figure 8-1). Toward this end, Microsoft retail stores actually offered a $100 credit to any consumers bringing in a Windows XP computer as a trade-in for newer, supported devices.[6]

[3]Ars Technica, Peter Bright, "Microsoft's Decision to Patch Windows XP Is a Mistake," http://arstechnica.com/security/2014/05/microsofts-decision-to-patch-windows-xp-is-a-mistake/, May 1, 2014.
[4]TechRepublic, Tony Bradley, "Windows XP Use Declining but Millions Still Willingly at Risk," www.techrepublic.com/article/windows-xp-use-declining-but-millions-still-willingly-at-risk/, April 16, 2014.
[5]Network World, "Twice as Many Desktops Still Running Windows XP than Windows 8, 8.1 Combined," www.networkworld.com/article/2226663/microsoft-subnet/twice-as-many-desktops-still-running-windows-xp-than-windows-8--8-1-combined.html, April 2, 2014.
[6]Daily Tech, Jason Mick, "Microsoft Will Give You $100 to Get Rid of Your Windows XP PC," www.dailytech.com/Microsoft+Will+Give+You+100+to+Get+Rid+of+Your+Windows+XP+PC/article34567.htm, March 21, 2014.

Figure 8-1. Microsoft developed a customized web site in 2013 to tell end users if their PC was in fact running Windows XP and, if so, how to upgrade. (Microsoft, amirunningxp.com)

Some corporations and government entities made exclusive, specific arrangements with Microsoft to pay for extended support of the operating system for a limited period of time, being unwilling or unable to switch their computers away from XP before the deadline. For example, the government in the United Kingdom agreed to pay Microsoft 5.5 million pounds (approximately $9.2 million in US dollars) to extend XP support for a single additional year.[7] The Internal Revenue Service also paid the company approximately $500,000 (significantly less than the figure originally cited by some sources) to extend Microsoft's support of its XP desktops for an additional year.[8] Big companies and government agencies with fear of being left unprotected can pay big money for a little more protection from Microsoft, for a short period of time.

---

[7]*Huffington Post*, Matthew Held, "If You're Still Using Windows XP Your Company Is at Risk," www.huffingtonpost.ca/matthew-held/windows-xp-no-support_b_5481600.html, June 10, 2014.
[8]*Computerworld*, Gregg Keizer, "Update: IRS Misses XP Deadline, Will Spend $30M to Upgrade Remaining PCs," www.computerworld.com/s/article/9247634/Update_IRS_misses_XP_deadline_will_spend_30M_to_upgrade_remaining_PCs, April 11, 2014.

But, for the average private consumer or small-to-medium business without the kind of deep pockets of the Internal Revenue Service or Britain, spending vast sums of money for continued support of an outdated operating system is simply not a realistic option. As time passes and April 2014 continues to recede further into the past, the list of Windows XP's weaknesses and vulnerabilities will grow larger and larger. Hackers will continue to find new avenues of attack and to share these exploits with others who will be both informed and emboldened by them. This list of weaknesses will never shrink, because Microsoft is no longer closing these security "holes." Windows XP is truly a "dead end." Any individual or entity still using XP is advised to immediately upgrade any XP machines still in use anywhere in their physical plant—whether a large corporation with thousands of machines, a smaller business with hundreds, a family business with several, or a private user with one. It also is critical to avoid using for any purpose an XP machine that belongs to someone else, like Sue from our introduction did—these devices simply can no longer be secured or relied on.

Ultimately, of course, the same fate will eventually befall all of Microsoft's other post-XP operating systems as well. These schedules have already been published for public consumption and infrastructure planning purposes. It takes time to retool the physical plant and associated communications infrastructure that large corporations (and governments) rely on to complete core operating tasks. Without advance warning of such OS impending abandonment, larger firms and individuals alike would be caught unaware and their data left vulnerable to attack. These published schedules go out years in advance. For example, Windows Vista is scheduled to go out of support in 2017, Windows 7 will go out of support in 2020, and Windows 8 will be unsupported in 2023. No one should be surprised when software products and the support systems they rely on for continued functionality are retired, yet many are.

Not Just Windows

Although we've focused primarily here on emergent vulnerabilities in the PC operating system context, this isn't a problem exclusive to Microsoft's operating systems. Apple also has moved to a yearly release schedule for new versions of its desktop operating system, OS X. The most recently announced version, OS X Yosemite, will go into distribution sometime in late 2014. Currently (mid-2014) the shipping version is the OS X 10.9 Mavericks. Apple actively supports the current version of the OS as well as the two most immediately previous versions, Lion and Mountain Lion. As of mid-2014, then, versions 10.7, 10.8, and 10.9 (the current shipping version) were actively being supported with security updates and patches. In February 2014 OS X 10.6, Snow Leopard, was removed from active support. This planned and explicitly scheduled support pullback left approximately 20 percent of Mac users (an estimated 15 to 20 million people) vulnerable to active exploits.[9] Average OS X users have upgraded to the newest operating system substantially more promptly than have Windows users, however. Within five months of its release, OS X 10.9 had an approximate 40 percent market share, with its predecessor, OS X 10.8, making up another 20 percent.[10] From these data, it appears that nearly two-thirds of Mac users are running one of the two most recent versions of the OS. Apple's OS upgrades are now free (as of version 10.8), which certainly helps to encourage more punctual user upgrades!

Not Just Operating Systems

Of course, in addition to the operating system that allows the device to function, all other software loaded on the machine must be updated and kept at a secure level of modernity. Browser plug-ins, such as Flash and Java, often are used as convenient avenues of attack by criminal hackers. Security analysts note that Java, produced by Oracle, has become criminals' favorite channel into users' PCs for an attack. For example, in December 2013, IBM's X-Force Threat Intelligence Report found that at least half of all exploits were aimed at Java.[11] Adobe's Reader software was a distant second at 22 percent of recorded exploits. Productivity software such as Microsoft Office also can be exploited. In November 2013, McAfee Labs discovered a threat that exploited the graphics-handling abilities of Microsoft Word. This vulnerability potentially allows an attacker to take over a computer by tricking users into opening an infected Word file.[12] What is clear is that the system protections offered through active updating and patching have across-the-spectrum data security relevance, and further speak to the importance of remaining current in all aspects of device functionality. From our story at the beginning of the chapter, Sue's parents' computer could easily have been infected by malware via exploits in Windows XP, Office 2007, both, or from exposure to another piece of outdated software.

---

[9]*Computerworld*, Gregg Keizer, "Apple Retires Snow Leopard from Support, Leaves 1 in 5 Macs Vulnerable to Attacks," www.computerworld.com/s/article/9246609/Apple_retires_Snow_Leopard_from_support_leaves_1_in_5_Macs_vulnerable_to_attacks, February 26, 2014.

[10]MacRumors, Eric Slivka, "OS X Mavericks Adoption Pushing Toward 50%," www.macrumors.com/2014/03/27/os-x-mavericks-adoption-50/, March 27, 2014.

[11]JavaWorld, Tony Bradley, "Report: Half of All Exploits Target Java," www.javaworld.com/article/2104862/java-security/report-half-of-all-exploits-target-java.html, March 5, 2014.

[12]McAfee.com, Haifei Li, "McAfee Labs Detects Zero-Day Exploit Targeting Microsoft Office," http://blogs.mcafee.com/mcafee-labs/mcafee-labs-detects-zero-day-exploit-targeting-microsoft-office-2, November 5, 2013.

Java updates have been particularly problematic, as many large organizations use other applications (database, HR, finance, etc.) that rely on specific versions of Java. These organizations may have customized their applications, relying on features in a specific Java version. When Java is upgraded, these customizations may not function as expected. So these companies are stuck with two unappealing choices: upgrade Java, and break existing functionality that might be mission-critical, or don't upgrade Java, leaving existing security vulnerabilities as venues of attack. In 2013, Oracle ruffled some feathers by using an update to Java version 7 to silently and forcibly remove Java version 6 from users' computers. This caused widespread failures of many companies' applications that depended on the older version.[13]

Not Just Desktops and Laptops

Here, again, it's not just the operating systems and software on desktops and laptops that are at risk as a consequence of obsolescence. The ubiquitous, powerful smartphones and tablets that are almost always in use and connected to the Internet also depend on software and applications that must be kept up-to-date. In Chapter 7 we discussed in depth the malware threats prevalent on the Android mobile operating system. A substantive contributing factor underlying these threats is the considerable "fragmentation" of that operating system's market. Apple's iOS is sold exclusively on hardware manufactured by Apple, in a monogamous hardware-software pairing. In contrast, the Android OS is made by Google but is sold on a range of hardware platforms. What this means is that there are many more versions of the Android operating system "in the wild," and the environment is consequently fragmented.

This also has led to a substantial percentage of users running operating systems that are increasingly clunky and out-of-date—way out-of-date. As of July 2014, 53 percent of the Android devices that had recently connected to the Google App Store were running Android version 4.1 or earlier (see Figure 8-2), which are from 2012 and earlier. Presuming this sample of users is reflective of the population of Android users broadly (and this may be a conservative assumption in light of their purchases of new software), this means that more than half of Android users are currently using operating systems that are at least two years old. In late 2013, Google announced the activation of its one billionth Android device. Taking into account the retirement of old devices and

---

[13]*Register*, John Leyden, "'Silent but Deadly' Java Security Update Breaks Legacy Apps-Dev," www.theregister.co.uk/2013/01/31/java_security_update/, January 31, 2013.

the purchase of new devices (Google claims 1.5 million Android devices are activated each day[14]), a conservative estimate puts at least 500 million Android devices running out-of-date system software. This is a really big target.

ANDROID VERSIONS (RELEASE DATE) MARKET SHARE, JULY 2014

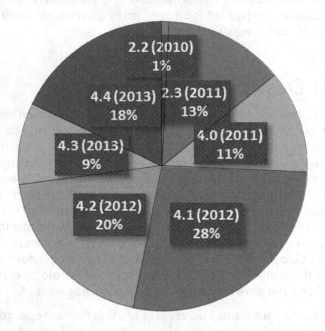

Figure 8-2. More than half of all Android devices, as of mid-2014, were still running operating systems from 2012 and earlier. (Data from http://developer.android.com/about/dashboards/index.html)

For all iOS devices, when a software or operating system update is released by Apple, the end user can decide when to install or make an upgrade. In contrast, on the Android platform, while the update is released by Google, the schedule is generally determined by the particular telecommunications provider (e.g., Sprint, Verizon, AT&T) supporting Internet access. The clear divide between these two approaches has led to essentially two classes of users:

---

[14]Pocket-lint, Elyse Betters, "1.5m Android Devices Activated Daily, 1 Billion Total Devices on Horizon," www.pocket-lint.com/news/122459-1-5m-android-devices-activated-daily-1-billion-total-devices-on-horizon, July 19, 2013

broadly protected and broadly unprotected. This divide may be at least in part a consequence of big business economics. Writing for *PC Magazine*'s "Security Watch," analyst Fahmida Rashid noted that:

> *Android's open platform allows device manufacturers and carriers to tweak the operating system to bundle extra software and set certain configuration settings. Whenever Google releases an operating system update, both the vendor and carriers have to test the changes against their homebrew systems before rolling out the latest version. The carriers claim this is a slow process, but many security experts believe carriers are prioritizing profit over security.* [15]

But the situation isn't entirely rosy on the other side of this divide either. Apple users are not wholly immune from vagaries in corporate data protection policy. For example, in February 2014 the company was criticized when a security fix was made available only for the newest OS (iOS 7) and not for the previous version of the system, iOS 6. [16]

At the time, approximately 15 percent of iPhone users were running the older version of the operating system. These users had chosen not to upgrade their software, many in response to reports of poor battery life when iOS 7 was installed on older hardware. Interestingly, Apple made a patch for iOS 6 available for users who were unable to upgrade to iOS 7. This included users of the iPhone 3GS, for example, as that device is not compatible with iOS 7. Here, in a conspicuous effort at social engineering, Apple drew a clear policy distinction between those users who couldn't upgrade their OS due to system incompatibility issues and those who chose not to upgrade due to performance issues (e.g., battery life). Users in the former category were supported with a security patch. Users in the latter were not, unless they relented and upgraded to the new software. The unseen hand at work....

In general, however, the immediacy of Apple's OS updates, coupled with the total homogeneity of the hardware appears to encourage iOS users to upgrade faster relative to Android users as a body. As shown in Figure 8-3, as of July 2014, the Apple Developer Program reported that 90 percent of active iPhones were running iOS 7, the most recent version of the operating system.

---

[15]*PC Magazine*, Fahmida Rashid, "Android's Biggest Security Threat: OS Fragmentation," http://securitywatch.pcmag.com/android/308966-android-s-biggest-security-threat-os-fragmentation, March 8, 2013.
[16]NPR, Laura Sydell, "iOS 6 Users Left in the Lurch After Security Flaw Discovered," www.npr.org/blogs/alltechconsidered/2014/02/25/282671039/ios-6-users-left-in-the-lurch-after-security-flaw-discovered, February 26, 2014.

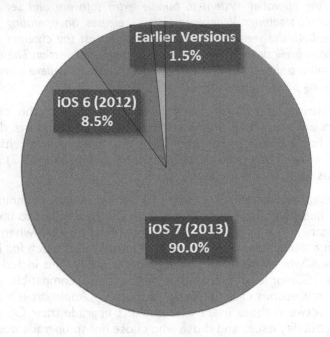

Figure 8-3. In general, iOS users upgrade their operating systems more regularly than Android users. (Data from https://developer.apple.com)

What Can You Do?

First, absolutely do not use Windows XP for anything. Period. Don't use a toaster in the bathtub…don't use Windows XP.

For all of your mobile devices, including phones and tablets, upgrade when new versions of the OS or a new patch are made available by the manufacturer. It is important to keep up with these upgrades serially as they're published. Adoption lags increase the potential that your devices will be vulnerable to attacks exploiting earlier system and software configurations. Often, however, as a result of emergent hardware insufficiencies, updates to the most current software or OS can no longer be made (e.g., iPhone 3GS ≠ iOS 7). If a device is old enough that it is no longer eligible for software updates, or is incompatible with the newest operating system, it may be worthwhile to consider investing in a new device.

This caution, of course, also applies to personal computers, be they Mac or Windows-based machines. Upgrade the operating system when a new version becomes public. Keeping operating systems and software current doesn't have to involve a lot of steps or take a lot of time. Users can take advantage of the automatic update option standard in all modern operating systems to automatically download new updates when these are announced. Given their favored status among criminals seeking access to your devices, it is also important to update software like Microsoft Office and Adobe Reader and browser plug-ins like Flash and Java, when these become available. Using outdated products for any length of time, particularly online, is just an invitation to hackers looking for easy points of access.

The mechanics of this process are obviously likely to be very different for personal computers vs. those owned and maintained by an employer. While users have autonomous control over their personally owned devices, on company computers many of the upgrade decisions are simply out of the hands of end users, who likely do not have extensive administrative privileges. Corporate or company IT departments generally set the upgrade policies that define the configuration of users' devices. Sometimes, there is a firm-level reason to stay with an older OS or software application. For example, a newer version of Java may not be compatible with an in-house database application or inventory management system, limiting the broad-scale options available for making an upgrade to current software. However, it is important that end users pay attention to upgrade e-mails and announcements from their corporate IT staff.

It is crucial that users try to actively collaborate with this process and adopt a regular, disciplined approach to keeping their devices up-to-date. Although tempting, because they can be annoying, don't try to find ways around automatic updates. Everyone groans when the message "Windows has new updates available that will require a reboot" pops up on their machine. But don't ignore these messages. Let the computer update itself ASAP. It is important not to wait if you believe your operating system, software application, or browser plug-in is out-of-date. Discuss these suspicions with your IT representative. It also is important not to connect any BYOD laptops, phones, or tablets to a corporate network or other resources if they are unpatched or at all out-of-date. Doing this has the potential to put the entire system or network at risk (and you won't know if the computer is out-of-date if it isn't yours). Increasingly, many corporate wireless networks will refuse to allow outdated computers or other devices (e.g., Windows XP computers) to connect to corporate resources.

Additional Reading

For more on keeping your systems up-to-date, see the following links and visit our web site at www.10donts.com/dinosaurs:

- Apple, "Updating OS X and Mac App Store Apps," a similar guide for Apple's operating system: http://support.apple.com/kb/ht1338

- Adobe, "Flash Player Help," a site that allows users to determine their current version of Flash and upgrade if necessary. It features comprehensive instructions for enabling it in your browser(s): http://helpx.adobe.com/flash-player.html

- Mashable, "Windows XP Isn't Safe to Use Anymore. Here's What to Do Next," a great guide helping users transition off of XP: http://mashable.com/2014/04/08/windows-xp-upgrade-or-switch/

- Microsoft, "What Is Windows Update?" a single point of reference for enabling automatic updates on each version of the Windows operating system: http://windows.microsoft.com/en-us/windows/windows-update

- Oracle, "Verify Java and Find Out-of-Date Versions," an easy way to determine if your computer uses an outdated version of Java: http://java.com/en/download/installed.jsp

Don't Trust Anyone Over... Anything

The Perils of Social Engineering

Darren is a newly hired financial analyst for a major e-retailing company with a background in database management, software integration, and big-data modeling. He was hired as part of a broadscale company reorganization following several recent acquisitions. Darren's group is part of a brand new unit within the parent company, with incompletely established functional boundaries. Four weeks into his new position, Darren is still learning the proper procedures, reporting relationships, colleagues' names, and general operating system parameters. Everything feels very up in the air for Darren—a very common feeling. He receives a phone call at work, which is purportedly from the IT help desk affiliated with his group. Although the caller ID on his desk phone may have indicated an external call, in the midst of a hectic moment Darren didn't notice.

The caller identifies herself to Darren as "Charlotte from the internal help desk," a reasonable call to expect given the circumstances. She tells Darren that IT staff are still working on provisioning his access to multiple internal systems that have not yet been completely configured for his new work group. This part of what the caller tells him is true. Each week Darren is gaining more access to new systems and databases necessary for his core work activities.

The caller "confirms" Darren's username/login ID, job title, and e-mail address and asks for his current password. Assuming the caller is legitimate (because she had all these other pieces of information), Darren provides her with his password without question—this is a mistake. It turns out that the caller was a spearphisher using social engineering as a first step in an APT (Advanced Persistent Threat) attack.

The attacker was aware of some changes and reorganization at Darren's company and the presence of new employees, more likely than not through intercepted e-mail traffic or information publicly available on social media. The attacker was able to leverage this partial information and intuition to trick Darren into providing her with critical additional information, such as systems passwords and logon credentials. Within a few days, Darren's genuine IT administrators notice multiple logins using his credentials from several sites worldwide. In response they disable his system access until the issue can be resolved, with the hope that no core infrastructure or company resources have been compromised in the interim—a slim hope at best.

What Is Social Engineering?

The term "social engineering" has seen attention in a number of domains, carrying distinct—even contradictory—meanings across these areas. In political science, for example, it refers to an elected leader or social group attempting to have a broad influence on public opinion over a specific set of issues bearing on the way that people live their lives (gay marriage, marijuana legalization, texting and driving, public smoking bans, etc.). This (or other) usage of the term is unrelated to its meaning in the information technology context we describe here. From an information technology/information security standpoint, social engineering refers to the wide range of social techniques that criminals use to "trick" users into unwittingly divulging confidential or proprietary data.

Targeted information can include personally identifiable information (PII), such as a social security number, birth date, mother's maiden name, favorite movie, name of elementary school, or any other "key" that vendors or employers ask users to supply to make themselves known to a controlled site. From our chapter opener, the attacker was seeking Darren's logon password.

PII can include financial information, such as a bank account number, checking account number, or credit card number, all of which position a criminal to begin digging toward a user's treasure. This can also include, as in our example with Darren, credentials for a work-related computer, web site, server, or any other electronic system or resource. Phishing, as discussed in Chapter 1, is the most commonly seen type of social engineering attack, but it is not the only type of attack.

Keep Your Eye on the Ball

Social engineering is often a first step in an orchestrated APT style of attack. Tricking an end user (or, even worse, a system administrator!) into providing organization credentials or other critical bona fides gives attackers their first crucial foothold into the architecture of an otherwise protected system. Effective social engineering requires that attackers gain as much information as possible about a target before making any kind of direct contact. If an attacker already has some (perhaps incomplete, perhaps disparate) pieces of information—a target's name, job title, login name, etc.—the target is much more likely to assume that the phone call, e-mail or text is legitimate. We saw this approach used with Darren at the beginning of the chapter. The caller knew Darren's username, e-mail address, and job title, and because she had these pieces of personal data it was much easier to manipulate him into providing her with critical information that she did not have—but needed—to execute an attack.

An attacker making contact "blind," with little or no personally identifying information, is unlikely to get very far with an even nominally sophisticated end user. Most (most!) users are unlikely to respond to an essentially random request over the phone or e-mail for their name, e-mail address, login name, or system credentials. However, if the caller already knows the user's name, has his e-mail address, and knows his login name, the victim is much more likely to provide his password. Unfortunately, users broadly assume that this kind of information is in some way protected (as they also broadly assume e-mail is a secure way to send information). From this incorrect assumption, it is an easy logical step to conclude that anyone who has this information must be an authority with rights to its access.

Transmitting an official personae to a targeted victim ("this is Charlotte from the help desk") is another core aspect underlying social engineering tactics. The key from the criminal's perspective is to get targets to believe that the communication is official. Effective social engineers speak with authority when calling a victim on the phone and adopt official-sounding prose when sending an e-mail. They can suggest indirectly or even explicitly frame their request for information as a time-critical situation. The goal with this time-driven approach is to press the target. If a victim is made to believe that the information request is urgent, and that speed is necessary to navigate a critical situation, this effectively limits the time the target has available to consider the ramifications of the decision to divulge sensitive information to the social engineer. If this has to be done "now," there is just no time to think about it.

Hooking the Phish

To generate presumptions of authority social engineers will attempt to put targets off balance. To do this, they may use phrases like "Don't you know who this is?" "Weren't you at the meeting where we discussed this issue with the senior members of your group?" "How long have you been with this section?" or "Haven't you been reading your e-mails?" This approach is likely to be particularly effective with new or inexperienced employees, like Darren from our chapter introduction, as they don't yet personally know the relevant players at the company or the standard protocol for delivering directives or collecting information. New employees also are often bombarded with information about new systems, new passwords, and new procedures in their first few weeks. More seasoned employees or employees with longer tenure are likely to be less susceptible (hopefully) to this approach.

Social engineering experts will aggressively use their knowledge of human psychology as a tool to gain access to the data that they are seeking. Criminals understand that they can often convince targets that they've got the right to access users' information if they can give the illusion that they actually already have it (or at least some of it). To accomplish this sleight of hand, they'll use phrases like "I just need you to confirm..." a certain piece of data, which implies that they already have the information they're seeking, even if they don't. They might prey on the inherently human desire to be helpful, and actively use the magic "please" and "thank you," cognizant of the old truism that "You can catch more flies with honey than with vinegar." But, they may approach a target from the opposite end of the spectrum. They might use scare tactics, telling end users that there is a very serious problem with their computer and that they need to cooperate before the issue worsens or leads to the "blue screen of death." They may even ask the user to type certain commands into the computer, with a real-time help desk or consulting ruse, which gives direct, real-time remote control over the computer to the attacker.[1] There are no social engineering tactics that criminals will not use to gain control over a target's computer; there are no out of bounds in the game or off-limits approaches.

Social Engineering via Social Networking

We live in a connected world, where we share our stories, our images, and many of the details of our daily lives with (often many) others we interact with only through computer-mediated communications technologies. We entrust these

[1]ZoneAlarm, "Beware of Social Engineering, a Scam Artist's Favorite Tool," www.zonealarm.com/blog/2014/01/beware-of-social-engineering-a-scam-artists-favorite-tool/, January 29, 2014.

personal details to the Internet and send them out. The profound prevalence, even ubiquity, of social networks has, in many ways, made it much easier for hackers trying to use social engineering tactics to spear-phish victims. This is an open secret.

Kevin Mitnick is a former hacker who spent five years in federal prison, convicted on federal wire fraud charges. He is now employed profession-ally as a security consultant. Asked how social media has changed hacking, he replies:

> *Made it easier. I can go into LinkedIn and search for network engineers and come up with a list of great spear-phishing targets because they usually have administrator rights over the network. Then I go onto Twitter or Facebook and trick them into doing something, and I have privileged access. If I know you love Angry Birds, maybe I would send you an e-mail purporting to be from Angry Birds with a new pro version. Once you download it, I could have complete access to everything on your phone.[2]*

Knowledge Is Power

Social networks provide criminals with an enormous amount of knowledge about the individuals connecting with other users through them. As we've consistently sought to highlight throughout this book, it is the human actors leveraging the technologies available today that are the weakest link in the cyber-security chain. Ninety-five percent of all successful cyber attacks are made possible by human error, according to IBM's 2014 Cyber Security Intelligence Index.[3] People share (and perhaps over-share) a great deal of personal information on Facebook, Twitter, Instagram, LinkedIn, and other social network sites. It is precisely this kind of information that criminals can (and do) use to design and build their social engineering attacks. The more information that's publicly available about a potential target, the more precise and detailed the attack can be.

Commercial firms often maintain active social media accounts for advertising and public relations purposes, and much of this information is available for broad public consumption. Details on upcoming company events, new hires, restructuring details, promotions, corporate social responsibility activities, etc. all may be regularly posted to social media, giving attackers a great deal of

---

[2]*Time*, Belinda Luscombe, "10 Questions for Kevin Mitnick," http://content.time.com/time/magazine/article/0,9171,2089344,00.html, August 29, 2011.
[3]*SC Magazine*, Marcos Colón, "'Human Error' Contributes to Nearly All Cyber Incidents, Study Finds," www.scmagazine.com/human-error-contributes-to-nearly-all-cyber-incidents-study-finds/article/356015/, June 16, 2014.

data around which to build a detail-rich attack. For example, reporting for Network World, security analyst Jan Buitron writes:

> *In an example provided by network infrastructure provider Terramark (with the victim company and employee names anonymized), hackers hijacked a Facebook account belonging to "Bob," a male employee at a financial institution, and sent a link to an unsuspecting female employee named "Alice" at the same firm. There had been a company picnic the previous weekend, and the e-mail from the hijacked account belonging to Bob promised pictures from the recent picnic. Alice clicked the link, expecting to see pictures of the company picnic. It appeared that nothing happened, but she had downloaded a keylogger onto her company laptop.[4]*

A keylogger, which is surveillance software (spyware), can record every keystroke made to a log file. The program can record the content of instant messages, e-mail, or any information typed using the keyboard. The log file created by the program can be sent to any IP address specified by the attacker. Some of these spyware programs can record e-mail addresses or web site URLs, also making all web activity and e-mail communications transparent to the attacker.

The attacker's knowledge of the recent company picnic allowed him to make the e-mail feel more personally authentic and believable to the recipient. Rather than being consigned to writing something along the lines of "Hey, here are some pictures you might like," an attacker is empowered to write the more believable and more compelling "Here are some great pictures of you from last weekend's picnic! You really look like you had fun!" This kind of plausible material inclusion increases the odds that the targeted victim will trust the legitimacy of the link embedded in the e-mail and then, unfortunately, as a consequence click the link. The target swallows the picnic bait, hook, line, and sinker, and the attacker bags a phish.

As we saw from the chapter opener, attackers can use publicly available information about company reorganizations, mergers, and other formal corporate changes to craft more effective attack vectors. The attacker who successfully deceived Darren knew that his company had recently undergone substantial organizational changes, which increased the likelihood that there would be more inexperienced employees to victimize. As we've tried to high-light throughout the book, successful digital criminals are opportunistic, and they systematically pursue the most accessible, uncomplicated targets with the highest probability of conversion.

---

[4]Network World, M. E. Kabay, "Social Engineering via Social Networking," www.networkworld.com/article/2237570/collaboration-social/social-engineering-via-social-networking.html, October 4, 2010.

Big Companies, Big Problems

This isn't a phenomenon to which only private users and small companies are falling prey. The results from a recently held security industry competition reveal that some of the world's largest, most well-known corporations continue to be plagued by incidents of employees simply handing out proprietary data over the phone to social engineering attackers. At the Defcon 2013 security conference, a competition called "Social Engineer Capture the Flag" was held to highlight the depth and pervasiveness of this problem.[5] Contestants, untrained social engineers, were selected to participate and were given a specific target company to "attack." The rules of the competition provided that the attackers were permitted to use only publicly available information from the company's web site and social media channels, such as Facebook and Twitter, to craft their attacks. The rules of the competition precluded the use of *any* "inside" information.

Even constrained in this way to the use of only public information, the Capture the Flag attackers were able to gain an enormous amount of information from the targeted companies. The kinds of critical information social engineering targets were willing to provide included what operating systems were used on their computers, the existence of corporate VPN (virtual private network) and wireless access, and information about the company's preferred vendors. The companies that performed better (i.e., their employees provided the Capture the Flag contestants with less information) did so not as a consequence of a disciplined adherence to strict data security protocol, but through ignorance alone (e.g., a newbie like "Darren" may simply not have had the information being sought by contestants). As Michele Fincher of Social-Engineer.inc., the contest organizer, reported, "The companies who happened to do well did so accidentally or out of ignorance in they either couldn't answer the question or didn't know how, so the call shut down. Very few said, 'I am not allowed to give out this information.'" The pattern of deep, concerning, porous data security observed in the 2013 event was not anomalous.

In the 2012 iteration of this conference, where a similar game of Capture the Flag was held, several large companies, including major worldwide players such as Wal-Mart and Target, were successfully "engineered" as well,[6] giving out vital security data to randomly chosen, untrained contestants over the phone. The data security chain that ultimately protects the credit card numbers, financial information, and personal identities of millions and millions of customers,

---

[5]We Live Security, Rob Waugh, "Big Companies Still Fall for Social Engineering "Hacks" by Phone—and It's Not Getting Better," www.welivesecurity.com/2013/10/31/big-companies-still-fall-for-social-engineering-hacks-by-phone-and-its-not-getting-better/, October 31, 2013.
[6]CNN, Stacy Cowley, "How a Lying 'Social Engineer' Hacked Wal-Mart," http://money.cnn.com/2012/08/07/technology/walmart-hack-defcon/index.htm, August 8, 2012.

even at large, publicly traded, multinational, multi-billion-dollar companies, ultimately is only as strong as the discipline of a single employee who's excited about pictures from last week's company picnic.

Ransomware

Social engineering crimes don't impact just the hacked company when the credit card databases at giant Fortune 500 retailers like Target, for example, are hacked.[7] These attacks can get extremely personal very, very fast, affecting a broad range of users' personal data beyond their credit card information (which is personal enough!). Ransomware is a category of malware often used in social engineering attacks that is based on defrauding end users. The first examples of ransomware actually appeared in the late 1980s and early 1990s, but the use of ransomware in social engineering has increased significantly over the last several years. The security firm AVAST reported that, during a six-week period in mid-2014, users visited ransomware-infected web sites more than 18 million times.[8]

As the aptly branded label suggests, this category of malware requires that users pay a ransom to "unlock" their computer or other device once it has been captured by an attacker. Early variants of ransomware, such as GPCode, Archiveus, and Cryzip, purported to lock users' computers until a ransom was paid, at which point an unlock code would be provided. In reality, however, the user's system was not actually rendered unusable by the infection. Early ransomware approaches often employed primitive forms of encryption. These could be easily repaired, and an updated anti-malware product or a skilled IT technician could successfully remove the infection.[9]

The game changed substantially in 2013 with the release of the "CryptoLocker" ransomware. Most typically delivered via malicious links embedded in e-mail messages, CryptoLocker actually does encrypt users' files with an extremely strong, unbreakable encryption. True to its forebears in style (though not functionality) the key to "unlock" or decrypt captured files, stored on servers controlled by the attackers, is held by the criminals until payment is made. Once a user's data are captured, a message is displayed on the user's computer

---

[7]*Bloomberg Businessweek*, Michael Riley, Ben Elgin, Dune Lawrence, and Carol Matlack, "Missed Alarms and 40 Million Stolen Credit Card Numbers: How Target Blew It," www.businessweek.com/articles/2014-03-13/target-missed-alarms-in-epic-hack-of-credit-card-data, March 13, 2014.

[8]avast! Blog, Jan Širmer, "Browser Ransomware Attacks Are Massive in Scale," http://blog.avast.com/2014/05/12/browser-ransomware/, May 12, 2014.

[9]TechRepublic, Michael Kassner, "Ransomware: Extortion via the Internet," www.techrepublic.com/blog/it-security/ransomware-extortion-via-the-internet/, January 11, 2010.

demanding a ransom payment. This ransom can typically be paid only using Bitcoin (an online-only currency), a MoneyPak voucher sent overseas, or some other difficult-to-trace method.

Generally the victim is given a calendar deadline, after which the encryption key is destroyed and the user's files left completely unrecoverable. Given the strength of modern encryption, stolen files really are most likely gone for good if the key is destroyed. However, even if the ransom is paid before the stipulated deadline, the attackers may or may not provide the correct decryption key. These are criminals unconstrained by established operational protocol. The defrauded user has no recourse if the decryption key is not released. Ultimately, there may be no way to recover encrypted data.

This is a growing problem: by late 2013 more than 30,000 computers worldwide had been infected by CryptoLocker alone, capturing the attention of larger players focused on limiting its spread.[10] The CryptoLocker threat was eased somewhat through the first half of 2014, as government agencies and Internet telecom providers blocked many of the servers the attackers were using to launch their attacks. In June 2014, the FBI actually seized many of the servers attackers had used to control CryptoLocker launches.[11]

While the CryptoLocker malware itself can be easily removed from any machine it has infected, the encryption had generally been unremovable (and files unrecoverable) without the key.[12] However, in August 2014, security companies FireEye and Fox-IT partnered to offer free recovery to any users who had files locked by CryptoLocker. Security researchers were able to obtain a copy of CryptoLocker's password database after the servers were seized by the FBI, allowing them to offer recovery services to affected users.[13]

---

[10]SecurityWeek, Ryan Naraine, "Cryptolocker Infections on the Rise; US-CERT Issues Warning," www.securityweek.com/cryptolocker-infections-rise-us-cert-issues-warning, November 19, 2013.

[11]*USA Today*, Donna Leinwand Leger and Kevin Johnson, "Federal Agents Knock down Zeus Botnet, CryptoLocker," www.usatoday.com/story/news/nation/2014/06/02/global-cyber-fraud/9863977, June 2, 2014.

[12]*Guardian*, Donna Ferguson, "CryptoLocker Attacks That Hold Your Computer to Ransom," www.theguardian.com/money/2013/oct/19/cryptolocker-attacks-computer-ransomeware, October 18, 2013.

[13]BBC, Mark Ward, "Cryptolocker Victims to Get Files Back for Free," www.bbc.com/news/technology-28661463, August 6, 2014.

Despite this partial reprieve, the nature of the ransomware threat has continued to evolve as the threat-counterthreat arms race cycle intensifies. Several variants of CryptoLocker have recently popped up, including Cryptowall[14] and Crilock.[15] In an effort to circumvent the structural constraints reflected in the direct attacks on the ransomware launch servers noted previously, these mutations adopt slightly different mechanisms of propagation. For example, rather than proliferating through e-mail, Crilock was designed to spread itself via either USB flash drive or peer-to-peer (P2P) networks, masquerading as an activation code or application for popular software such as Microsoft Office and Adobe Creative Suite. Again, we encourage users to avoid downloading or even looking for software that they haven't paid for—the risks of secondary data loss are just too great.

The risks associated with this virulent epidemic are not exclusive to computers. Ransomware can easily infect mobile devices such as tablets and smartphones as well. In an ominous, unholy marriage, the developers of this category of malware have begun using social engineering tactics to convince their victims to pay the ransom. In May 2014, a new version of ransomware called Koler.A was discovered. Designed to infect the Android operating system, this malware is spread through pornography sites. The ransom notice sent to victims of the attack informs users that they have been browsing illegal pornography and must immediately pay or they will be reported to the proper authorities.[16]

Although the users may have been browsing perfectly legal pornography (for their jurisdiction), in light of the sensitive nature of the online activity, this kind of ransom notice has the potential to be extremely effective at frightening users into compliance with ransom demands. Koler.A demands a $300 ransom from users to decrypt their files, but the ransom demand is entirely bogus. The files are not actually encrypted, and the malware is relatively simple to remove. But, because the ransomware infects only Android users visiting pornography sites, these users may be more vulnerable to the social engineering within which the ransom demand is framed.

---

[14]Cyberoam, "Cryptowall—the Extended Version of Cryptolocker," www.cyberoam.com/blog/cryptowall-the-extended-version-of-cryptolocker/, June 12, 2014.
[15]Trend Labs, Abigail Pichel, "New CryptoLocker Spreads via Removable Drives," http://blog.trendmicro.com/trendlabs-security-intelligence/new-cryptolocker-spreads-via-removable-drives/, December 25, 2013.
[16]*Guardian*, Stuart Dredge, "Android Porn Browsers Warned to Watch out for Koler.A Ransomware," www.theguardian.com/technology/2014/may/08/android-porn-koler-a-ransomware, May 8, 2014.

In-Person Tricks

It isn't only users of the Internet who are vulnerable to these kinds of threats. Social engineering approaches aren't limited to remote or virtual attacks launched through e-mails, phone calls, and social network sites. Surprisingly, social engineering attacks also can be—and are—regularly perpetrated face-to-face. This is an extremely pervasive problem. Criminals posing as IT staff or other communications infrastructure technicians may be able to bluff their way past receptionists, security guards, and other official gatekeepers if they "act the part" and project confidence, seemingly authorized to be there.

Newer employees like "Darren" in the first months of employment at a particular organization, or employees working for companies going through any kind of physical reorganization, are clearly most vulnerable to in-person social engineering. They may not know the names or even the faces of the key personnel responsible for the physical maintenance of their company's communications infrastructure. As with virtual social engineering, the inclusion of a few bits of well-positioned plausible material increases the odds that the targeted victim will take the criminal's identity for granted. An official-looking name badge and a confidently delivered "I just talked to Suzanne and Mark at the help desk about the work order for this group…" go a long way when the new guy doesn't know who Suzanne or Mark are, or even where the help desk is.

This kind of brazen attack is happening in more and more companies. In 2010 two men posing as painters were able to steal a number of computers from two Philadelphia schools.[17] The attackers boldly entered the buildings, seemingly part of the background preparation for the start of the fall term, and walked out with thousands of dollars-worth of hardware. In 2013, a dozen men were arrested in London for an "audacious" attack on one of the country's largest banks. Posing as an IT engineer, one of the criminals attached a key logging device to a computer at a bank branch, which could have enabled the team to control the bank's computers from a remote location and steal millions of dollars from the branch.[18] These are not isolated incidents. In Ohio in 2014, a criminal posing as a Time Warner technician was able to gain access to people's homes, physically attaching a device to their home network infrastructure.[19] These startling examples represent merely

---

[17]Philly.com, Martha Woodall, "Pair Posing as Painters Steal Computers from Philadelphia Schools," http://articles.philly.com/2010-07-31/news/24971378_1_computer-thefts-imac-desktop-computer-schools, July 31, 2010.
[18]BBC, "Arrests over "Cyber Plot" to Steal from Santander Bank," www.bbc.com/news/uk-england-london-24077094, September 13, 2013.
[19]13ABC, Christine Long, "Sheriff Warns of Man Posing as Time Warner Worker in Monclova Twp.," http://www.13abc.com/story/26015883/sheriff-warns-of-man-posing-as-time-warner-worker-in-monclova-twp, July 14, 2014.

the tip of the iceberg. What's clear is that criminals are both willing and able to literally walk right in off the street and take on the identity of anyone in a position of authority in order to walk off with the goods.

It is human nature to want to be helpful and to assume that people are telling you the truth. But in a world where criminals are focused on stealing our money and our identity, a little healthy skepticism can provide a barrier to protect against becoming the victim of a practiced thief. Attackers can prey on people's innate helpfulness to introduce a keylogger, Trojan, or other malicious software into a company's network. An attacker might pose as a job candidate and ask a friendly receptionist to please print out a copy of his résumé, as he left his behind in the taxicab. He hands his USB thumb drive to the receptionist, and, when plugged in, the program infects that computer (and the rest of the company's network as well).[20]

Not Your Mother's Kind of Tailgating

Normally well-secured areas in a physical plant can often be easily bypassed by practiced social engineers as well. "Tailgating" refers to the practice of an unauthorized person following someone else (who is authorized) through a secured door or other passage into a secured area. Again, human nature and general friendliness play a role here. Most people will tend to hold the door for someone else and not close it in that person's face. This pattern holds true whether the door is to a secured area or a nonsecured one and whether or not the first person is acquainted with the second person or knows her authorized status for that area. If tailgating attackers project confidence and act like they are "supposed to be there" (rather than slinking around suspiciously) this increases their chances of success.[21]

How to Combat Social Engineering

Again, as with many of the security risks and tactics that we describe throughout this book, effectively combating social engineering scams comes down at least in part to adopting a little bit of healthy paranoia when it comes to your data, your devices, and your identity (either personal or professional). Remember that no reliable organization (your employer, your bank, your credit card company) should *ever* ask you for a password over the telephone.

---

[20] Vice, Angela Hennessy, "We Spoke to a Social Engineer About How He Hacks People and Infiltrates "Secure" Companies," www.vice.com/en_ca/read/we-spoke-to-a-social-engineer-about-how-he-hacks-people-and-infiltrates-secure-companies, July 9, 2013.

[21] Lifehacker, Alan Henry, "How to Convince Someone You Work in Their Building," http://lifehacker.com/5854086/how-to-convince-someone-you-work-in-their-building?tag=socialengineering, November 15, 2012.

This is simply a ploy invented by criminals seeking to profit through your better nature. Be extremely suspicious of any kind of vague or generic identifiers on the phone: "This is your bank," "This is the IT department," "This is your regional director," "This is your supervisor's office manager," etc. If the person on the other end of the call cannot provide you with a name or a brand you recognize, don't provide the caller with any information at all. Call back using a phone number that you personally know and trust.

In person, if you don't recognize someone as being an individual with official status or as an established authority, ask a supervisor or another trustworthy source. It is always better to be skeptical when you are uncertain—someone who is supposed to be there or have access to your information will understand your uncertainty and will more likely than not respect you for displaying caution. Don't let someone into a secure area if you don't know for certain that he or she is allowed to be there; be cautious, be skeptical, and don't make a mistake in an effort to be polite to someone you don't know. Secure areas are secure for a reason. Although this is likely to strike our readers as naive in light of Internet usage trends among our target demographic, don't overshare personal or work-related information on social media, particularly with strangers.

This is a bad habit that many of us have, and it creates inherent personal and financial vulnerabilities that carry real costs. Don't look for or download software available on sketchy sites or P2P networks. It is always much better to pay retail and be sure that what you've got is the real thing (with no bugs). If you've made some unfortunate choices, or been hit in the crossfire as a bystander in a broadscale attack, and your machine seems to be infected with ransomware, immediately consult with your IT staff or other experts before paying any demanded ransom. Paying ransom can complicate any entanglement with a social engineer and may only result in a loss of your money. There is no guarantee that a social engineer will give back your data once funds have been sent.

Additional Reading

For more on how to keep yourself safe from social engineers, see the following links and visit our web site at www.10donts.com/trust:

- Dell SecureWorks, "Prevent Social Engineering from Compromising Your Security", an explanation of social engineering from the perspective of Dell's security consultant subsidiary: www.secureworks.com/consulting/security_testing_and_assessments/social_engineering/

- Cisco Systems, "Protect Against Social Engineering", a look at social engineering prevention from a system administrator angle, but end users will find some useful hints as well: www.cisco.com/web/about/security/intelligence/mysdn-social-engineering.html

- Lifehacker, "How Can I Protect Against Social Engineering Attacks?", an informal exploration of the topic, with links to other detailed articles: http://lifehacker.com/5933296/how-can-i-protect-against-hackers-who-use-sneaky-social-engineering-techniques-to-get-into-my-accounts

- Panda Security, "How Does Social Engineering Work?", A simple explanation of the concept, and why it's such a threat: www.pandasecurity.com/mediacenter/security/social-engineering/

- Social Engineer, Inc's home page, a free resource for learning more about social engineering tactics and how to combat them: www.social-engineer.org/

- US Computer Emergency Readiness Team (US-CERT), "Avoiding Social Engineering and Phishing Attacks", An official government explanation of the threat, and how to combat it: www.us-cert.gov/ncas/tips/ST04-014

Don't Forget the Physical

We Are (Still) Living in a Material World

Tanya is the senior gastroenterological fellow at a large private hospital in a medium-sized city in the Northwest. As a physician working for a large, diverse practice, she is well versed in the protection of medical data, HIPAA (Health Insurance Portability and Accountability Act), and similar medical records–keeping regulations intended to help preserve the privacy of patients' personal medical data. In order to maintain up-to-date patient records, which takes her hours at the end of each workday, Tanya has a work laptop computer she uses at home that connects her to the hospital's servers via a VPN (virtual private network), which is completely secure

The laptop is immediately protected by a password any time the lid is closed and reopened, or after ten minutes of inactivity, as required by the hospital's IT policy. An additional requirement of the policy is that no one else is allowed to use her work laptop. Because of these non-employee-use constraints, Tanya and her family (husband and two kids) have a desktop computer at home.

Tanya's kids primarily use the computer for games and social networking, while Tanya and her husband also use it to pay bills, check Facebook, etc. They all use the computer together and share it. Because the computer is their "home" computer, it has no password enabled and no "inactivity period" after which the screen locks itself. One month, while reconciling bank accounts and credit card bills, Tanya notices some charges from Amazon that she doesn't remember making.

When she checks with her husband and kids, it turns out that they didn't make the charges either. After consulting with Amazon, MasterCard, and the issuing bank, Tanya discovers that it was a baby-sitter who watched their kids a couple of times who had ordered several things illegally from Amazon. Their unsecured home computer had files containing important financial information, including their credit card numbers and checking account. The baby-sitter was able to use one of those credit card numbers to place orders for herself with the giant web retailer.

The teenage baby-sitter's parents agreed to reimburse Tanya for the unauthorized charges, and neither Tanya nor MasterCard elected to press charges against the underage thief. The losses ultimately were relatively small, but Tanya recognized that the situation could have been much worse. After discussing the problem with the IT experts at the hospital, Tanya realized that her computer should always be locked when there's even a remote possibility that someone other than her family might gain physical access to her property.

Physical Security: An Overview

Although our discussion to this point has been overwhelmingly focused on emergent virtual threats, it is essential not to lose sight of the fact that we are living in a material world (nod to Madonna), which requires taking steps to ensure the physical security of data and property. Perhaps elementary in some respects—even increasingly taken for granted as our senses are trained more on virtual threats—physical security involves protecting actual devices— phones, tablets, laptops, desktops, Bluetooth equipment, data storage tools (disks, thumb drives)—from use by unauthorized actors who would steal property and treasure.

Today, most people's attention is almost exclusively on virtual security, and for good reason—the ways in which we operate today require vigilant attention to digital security issues. We've discussed digital security extensively throughout this book: how attackers can and unfortunately often do gain access to your data remotely, for example, has been a recurrent theme that is absolutely relevant for millions of users today.

But if attackers (and this includes fairly middle-of-the-road, amateur attackers like Tanya's baby-sitter) can physically get their hands on your device(s), without any (or with only rudimentary) password protection or other security gates in place, you've made their job much easier. Physical security of information technologies aims to prevent attacks, and ultimately potentially catastrophic data losses, from occurring primarily along two major vectors.

The first is actual theft of the apparatus, where the device is physically removed from the premises. Physical theft obviously results in the loss of the equipment itself (which in some cases can represent a substantial financial cost) and also—and in most cases more important—puts all of the data stored on the device at risk of loss. This can include, of course, not only sensitive financial and personal data, but also passwords and other means of authentication to social networks as well as proprietary professional databases.

The second is unauthorized usage, as with Tanya's baby-sitter. Here, while the physical equipment itself isn't stolen outright, it is substantively compromised through surreptitious use by an unauthorized person (or persons) for his or her own purposes without permission. While in this case there is no immediately obvious financial cost associated with the loss of equipment per se, the ultimate risk of data loss (and potential unauthorized access to social networks and downstream professional resources) actually may be substantially greater than the vulnerability present in the equipment theft scenario. A user who is unaware of unauthorized use of (or access to) her device(s) has no reason to take precautionary steps, notify anyone in authority of a security breach, or stop using the machine herself for data storage or to access networks or other potentially vulnerable critical resources. Access is achieved in stealth.

An attacker may have installed a keylogger or other malware on the system, enabling long-running, persistent access to a user's data and all of the other data vulnerable through the device. Just as a deeply embedded spy with top security clearance, who also is a Rotary Club officer, has kids on the school soccer team, and plays three-handicap golf in the charity fund-raiser, can feed secrets to a hostile country for years, when a computer is infiltrated in secret no one suspects any danger until it is too late.

In this chapter, with what at first blush may seem like a sepia-toned 20th-century importance placed on object permanence, we focus on physical security considerations in three primary areas of vulnerability that constitute the domains of use for all information and communication technologies. These are physical security at home, at work, and on the road or other public locations. We were hard-pressed to think of any instances ultimately not encompassed by activities occurring in these three domains. Our goal here is to offer a comprehensive domain-specific overview of the approaches associated with enhanced physical security of information and communication technology.

Physical Security at Home

Most of us spend most of our time at home, where we also spend a great deal of time using sophisticated digital devices that connect us to work, friends, and Internet-enabled activities. Today, with flexible work arrangements, contract work, 24-hour connectivity policies, etc., many of us may actually be at least as connected while at home as at work. At home, we want to keep our data protected both from old-school criminals who might (on extremely rare occasions) break in, and from any others (invited by us or not—here read kids' friends, baby-sitters, service professionals, maintenance personnel, spouses of friends, etc.) who while essentially authorized to be in our homes are *not* in any way authorized to access our digital devices or personal data.

As a brief aside, although an in-depth treatment of home security (i.e., keeping criminals out) is clearly outside the scope of this book, it is important to be aware that digital tools available today are making it much easier for criminals to gain unauthorized physical entry to your home. For example, broadly accessible smartphone software now exists that facilitates the near-instantaneous digital copying of the physical key to someone's front door. With access to a house key for less than 30 seconds (e.g., drop your keys at the door for a designated driver, drop your keys with the valet at the restaurant), apps such as KeyMe can make a digital record, and a physical copy can then be created at a later time, allowing unauthorized access to the home.[1] So, continuing the aside, be careful when handing over your keys to anyone—people at work, a valet at a restaurant, etc.—because it might mean that you're also putting the security of your home at risk.

Letting Outsiders In

We all have the occasional need to grant authorized access to our homes to individuals other than our friends and immediate family. Not you? This set of acceptable strangers and service providers can include anyone from nannies and baby-sitters to landlords, contractors, landscapers, caterers, pool cleaners, repair people, electricians, plumbers, realtors, painters, pet sitters, cleaning companies, the cable guy, and pest control. Although we often think of our homes as private places, in reality we actually grant access to them to a wide range of people we really know very little about, except what we might find on Craigslist or learn from an advocates' blog.

Sometimes, perhaps more often than not, these individuals are in our homes without any direct supervision from us. How much time do you actually spend sitting and watching the plumber or the pest control professional or installer at work? Are you really always hovering over the shoulder of the multiple members of the cleaning crew that comes to your home three times a month or the electrician or the cable guy as they, respectively, clean your house, put in new services, or repair your systems? We leave these professionals alone to do their work. As a consequence, they're essentially autonomous, with basically unfettered access within our private living spaces. More likely than not, while they're working we're doing our own work so we don't lose a day of productivity away from the office. A lot of the time, we may not even be at

---

[1] *Wired*, Andy Greenberg, "The App I Used to Break into My Neighbor's Home," www.wired.com/2014/07/keyme-let-me-break-in/?mbid=social_fb, July 25, 2014.

home when an authorized person comes in to do something we've paid him to do. A landlord, pet sitter, property manager, or contractor, for example, may need to come into a home while the residents are away at work. Sometimes, residents are present for part but not all of the time an authorized visitor is present. A baby-sitter, for example, may have some unsupervised time in the home after the children go to sleep but before the parents return.

Obviously this caution is in no way intended to undermine the valued relationships developed with service providers and caregivers over years of loyal service. We all have a certain level of trust that we've invested in these individuals that allows us to give them access to our homes (or our children!) in the first place. But another theme we've returned to again and again throughout this book is that a healthy dose of paranoia is the best way to protect our digital assets from compromise or theft. Yes, the baby-sitter is wonderful with the children and they adore her, the electrician does great work and was recommended by a friend, and the cleaning crew leaves your home feeling like it did when you first moved in. Although these authorized persons may consistently provide you with great service and make your life so much easier, this doesn't necessarily mean that given the opportunity they wouldn't also poke around through your private files or attempt to make unauthorized use of your unsecured financial assets. Don't tempt them!

Removing Temptation

The best way to protect your digital data at home is to take some of the same kinds of precautions as you'd take in the office. Home computers should always be protected with a password, and one that isn't written down on a sticky note next to the keyboard! All computers should be set to require the entry of a password after a certain interval of inactivity has passed, preferably a relatively short interval such as no more than 10 to 15 minutes. This substantially limits the window of opportunity available to anyone inadvertently coming into contact with a device he or she is not authorized to access. If Tanya's machine had been locked down in this way, it wouldn't have been a temptation to her baby-sitter.

Although this next step carries with it the trade-off inherent in the tenuous balance between security and convenience we've iterated several times in earlier chapters, with computers shared by the members of a family, it is sound data security policy always to maintain different passwords for each user. This approach provides that the kids (or the baby-sitter supposedly supervising their time spent on the computer) don't have access to all of their parents' files, passwords, account numbers, etc., and the parents can't mess up their kids' music-share files or on-going saved games. (Parents should, however, probably know their kids' usernames and passwords in case someone's homework gets lost or in the event of another emergency).

Not only does this kind of explicit user segregation protect against kids accidentally (or criminals intentionally) gaining access to important data that they shouldn't have access to in the first place, it also protects against their accidentally deleting something critical saved on the machine that could otherwise be irrevocably lost. In this same vein, all mobile devices, such as iPads, tablets, minis, smartphones, etc., also should be protected with a password or a PIN. None of these devices should be left out in the open when an authorized stranger is expected to be in the home without supervision, as they make very tempting targets both for unauthorized access to data and for actual physical theft!

Don't Blanket the Neighborhood with Wi-Fi

As we noted in Chapter 5, because liberal or uncontrolled access to a network can also lead to a loss of security, home Wi-Fi routers should be secured with a strong password. Because of the inherently porous boundaries, it is important to consider very carefully if you want to give the password to your Wi-Fi out to non–family members such as baby-sitters or other guests in your home. Social pressures to be virtually accommodating notwithstanding, once your password is out there's really no telling into whose hands it can fall. One solution to this potentially touchy issue of etiquette is a dual-network system: one "public" and one "private." Toward this end, many wireless routers actually allow for the maintenance of two networks simultaneously.[2] The first is the "primary" network, which is protected by a strong password with access to all of the devices on the network. The second is the "guest" network, which may or may not have a password, and which allows access only to the Internet, but not to any other computers or other devices in the home connected to the network.

To avoid the discomfort and social stress associated with having to tell a guest in your home or an employee, "Sorry, I can't give you my username and password because I'm worried you might steal from me" or "We only give out our Wi-Fi password to friends and family we trust, and you're not either…," consider as an alternative setting up a guest network. This will allow your visitors and employees access to only that segregated network. But, make sure that the password to the guest network is different from the password used on your primary network! If you do allow guests access to your primary (or only) Wi-Fi network, think carefully about the password you use for the network. Because you'll be giving this password out to other people, make sure it's not the same password that you also maintain to log on to your computer, your bank accounts, your corporate e-mail, etc. And, if it is the same password, change it!

---

[2]How-to Geek, "How to Enable a Guest Access Point on Your Wireless Network," www.howtogeek.com/153827/how-to-enable-a-guest-access-point-on-your-wireless-network/.

It is important to note that in the case of wireless access, you should account not only for contractors or other service providers who have access to the interior of your home, but also for those individuals who work on the exterior of your home or elsewhere on your property, including landscapers, pool technicians, painters, and the like. The typical home-use wireless router has a coverage radius of approximately 150 feet when placed inside a home, so potential access to your data does not end at the front door (see Figure 10-1).[3] Be careful that you're not extending your Wi-Fi network too far into your neighbor's home, particularly if you live in a condo or apartment. Most wireless routers intended for home usage feature the ability to "dial back" transmitting power as a way to limit the range of the device.

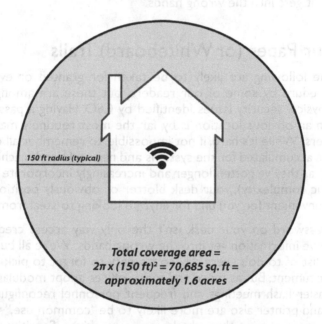

150 ft radius (typical)

Total coverage area =
$2\pi \times (150\ ft)^2 = 70{,}685$ sq. ft =
approximately 1.6 acres

Figure 10-1. The 150-foot radius of typical home wireless access points gives a maximum coverage area of more than an acre and a half, so exterior visitors to a home must be considered as well

---

[3]About.com, Bradley Mitchell, "What Is the Range of a Typical Wi-Fi Network?" http://compnetworking.about.com/cs/wirelessproducts/f/wifirange.htm.

Physical Security at Work

Maintenance of physical security at work carries with it a different set of constraints. At the office, many of the decisions users would otherwise make autonomously are made by IT or other security personnel and not by the typical end user (this will, of course, vary to a certain extent as a function of user expertise and work policy). Despite this shift in the burden of physical security responsibility, it is still critical that end users be cognizant of—and remain vigilant to—some basic tenets of physical security. *CSO Online* magazine points out that "Desks and other work spaces often have items on or around them that contain sensitive information, and that information can be dangerous if it gets into the wrong hands."[4]

Limit Your Paper (or Whiteboard) Trails

Some of the following are likely to be taken for granted or even seen as default procedure by some of our readers, but these are among the most common physical security issues identified by CSO. Having a password written down in an obvious location is by far the most routinely made security error by users. While it's hard, if not impossible, to remember all of the passwords we've accumulated for the systems and networks and machines we use (particularly as they've gotten longer and increasingly incorporate heightened alphanumeric complexity), your desk blotter or obviously positioned Post-it notes are convenient for you *and* for anyone looking to steal from you.

Leaving a password on your desk isn't the only way access credentials and other sensitive information get into the wrong hands. We're all busy and have a mile-long list of to-do's every day, so it's easy to forget to pick up a fax or a printed document. But as more and more offices adopt modular configurations for easier flash meetings and frequent personnel reconfigurations, the copier, fax, and printer also are more likely to be "common use," with everyone's documents coming through the same machines. Sensitive documents (with clear identifiers) left in a nonprivate printer, copier, or fax machine are among the top of the list of physical security vulnerabilities opportunistic thieves take advantage of today.

The way we work is constantly changing. Among the most prevalent (and frustrating!) modern conventions we all face is the ubiquitous meeting. Here, we impart the cutting edge to the members of the potentially numerous teams we all belong to through collective sharing of written documentation in

---

[4]*CSO Online*, Joan Goodchild, "6 Desk Security Mistakes Employees Make Every Day," www.csoonline.com/article/2112409/employee-protection/6-desk-security-mistakes-employees-make-every-day.html, January 23, 2009.

common work spaces with porous boundaries. Writing sensitive information on a conference room whiteboard during a meeting and leaving it there after the meeting breaks up is among CSO's top prescriptions for data loss. Who wants to stand there erasing the whiteboard while everyone else is walking out the door? Surely someone else will do that, right? Sometimes, no one does, leaving thieves with access to otherwise privileged, sensitive information.

Whether you're a team manager, a facilities supervisor, a regional director with broad employee oversight responsibilities, or you work in a small office with a flatter vertical configuration, making sure that physical security policies are enforced is essential. This has to start with just getting the word out so employees know what to do—and what not to do (e.g., no one's going to look at the Post-its on my machine). Everyone you work with who comes into contact with any kind of core-process data should be aware of the security policies and procedures governing their handling (if there are any!) and should adopt these as baseline physical security behavior.

Keep Company Devices Secured and Keep Them out of the Wrong Hands

Many organizations today maintain strict policies governing locked doors, unattended devices, and entry protocol. Many also require the regular use of "Kensington cables" or other devices that physically secure a laptop to a desk, wall, or other immovable surface. These anchor cables require a key to unlock the device before it can be moved. But, as with passwords written down on Post-its stuck to a computer monitor, in order to be an effective deterrent against theft the Kensington key must stay on the user's person and not be left in the lock, in the drawer, or on the desk! Physical anchoring is clearly not a foolproof approach, being subject to the ongoing convenience-security trade-offs that all users make every day. When properly used, laptop security cables can delay a thief long enough to be spotted or, because of deterrent frustration, lead a thief to a less well-protected potential target.

At work, where we often don't know everyone in our own offices and certainly don't know everyone who comes through the door either regularly or randomly, it is important to be extremely cautious when allowing any non-employee (e.g., contractor, visitor, speaker, applicant for a position, someone you don't recognize) to use any company-owned device. Security policy in some organizations may forbid this kind of sharing altogether, no exceptions. In organizations where some equipment sharing is permitted, any kind of computer use should be fully supervised. Critical here, the use of any noncompany devices, such as USB flash drives, should be totally forbidden. As discussed in Chapter 9, vehicles such as USB flash drives can easily be employed to introduce potentially fatal malware into a corporate network with devastating consequences.

Visitors, guests, or other noncompany personnel in need should be shown courtesy and should be provided with help in whatever way safely possible. Computers in public locations that are intended for guests' use should be configured by IT staff with minimal access to sensitive domains. These should also be regularly scanned for malware infections, and employees should never use these public computers for any of their core work activities, sending data, printing, or accessing company databases or other resources. In order to help maintain physical security, employees also should be very hesitant to lend access to their personal cards or keys to other employees or (particularly) guests to the office—restroom key or other. A smartphone app and 30 seconds are all that are necessary to copy a key. If your keys are out of your sight and in someone else's control for 30 seconds or more they could very easily be digitally copied.

Physical Security on the Road

Finally, it is a reality of modern life we're all too familiar with that a great deal of our work is accomplished on the road. More than ever, beyond work, we also have become a traveling society that vacations abroad as well. Laptop and other mobile device theft including phones and tablets has become a major (and extremely expensive!) problem for travelers and the companies they work for. For example, in a 2011 Ponemon Institute study sponsored by Intel Corporation,[5] it was reported that laptop theft cost US companies upwards of $2.1 billion per year, while European companies lost almost that much to theft, $1.8 billion per year. Consistent with the recurrent themes throughout this book, it is estimated that the physical equipment losses amounted to only about 20 percent of the total lost to theft. Ponemon estimated that the remaining 80 percent of the lost billions were spent dealing with the operational aftermath of stolen data: reclaiming lost network security, reconstituting compromised databases, reconfiguring proprietary operational processes. In some respects, oddly coherent with a very 21st-century reality, the hundreds of millions of dollars in physical property losses can be thought of as incidental.

---

[5]*InformationWeek*, Mathew J. Schwartz, "Lost Laptops Cost $1.8 Billion Per Year," www.informationweek.com/mobile/lost-laptops-cost-$18-billion-per-year/d/d-id/1097314?, April 21, 2011.

Thieves Are Everywhere

These physical losses are occurring overwhelmingly while employees are not at their desks (although, as noted previously, on-site physical plant losses are still a major problem). Companies in the United States reported that 43 percent of employees' laptops were lost off-site, at another physical plant, and 33 percent of these were lost in transit.[6] These statistics should leave no doubt that physical security on the road is a major, ongoing, complex, and expensive issue.

Airports are among the primary points of vulnerability for laptop theft (see Figure 10-2). We're running to catch a plane, trying to make a connection, eating on the go, waiting in line, waiting for a bag, running to the restroom, checking flight information, trying to get through. Our senses are bombarded by people and moving and transitions and canned air and music and uncomfortable seats and indigestion, and our guard gets worn down in the process. We're vulnerable because of our distraction. We're targets, and there are a lot of us in close proximity to choose from while we're in transit.

TOP LAPTOP THEFT AREAS IN AIRPORTS

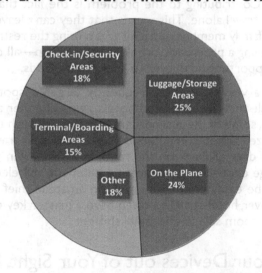

Figure 10-2. Laptops are at risk at many points along the typical traveler's pathway. (Data from http://blogs.absolute.com/lojack-for-laptops/2013/09/top-5-laptop-theft-areas-in-airports/).

---

[6]Intel, "The Billion Dollar Lost Laptop Problem," www.intel.com/content/www/us/en/enterprise-security/enterprise-security-the-billion-dollar-lost-laptop-problem-paper.html, October 31, 2010.

As Absolute Software, the makers of LoJack digital laptop tracking software, reports, airports represent a perfect storm of conditions conducive to the loss of property. The company writes, "Airports have a concentration of people traveling with laptops and other devices, often juggling multiple bags in crowded situations and unfamiliar surroundings. The combination of factors gives thieves many opportunities to walk away with unattended devices."

What's more, we go into these situations essentially broadcasting what's inside our luggage. Laptop bags and carrying cases are generally fairly easily identifiable because of their shape. An experienced thief can distinguish bags that are likely to contain expensive computer equipment from those carrying our toiletries and dirty laundry. In some ways, the procedures that are intended to increase passenger safety conspire to increase the transparency of what we've got in our bags. In the United States, Transportation Security Administration (TSA) rules require that laptops be removed from most carrying cases at the embarkation security checkpoint. At a glance, a professional thief can identify the more expensive and desirable models going through the scanner and target those laptops. A thief also may look for a laptop with any kind of identifying sticker from a bank, hospital, or other organization and specifically target those machines. Contributing to the problem is the fact that most business travelers tend to travel alone. This means that they can't leave their laptop or other bag with a family member or friend when using the restroom, purchasing food or drink, buying a paperback, or taking a quick nap—all of which provide an opening for opportunistic thieves to snatch the goods.

Hotels also are a very dangerous, frequently targeted spot for laptop and tablet theft. While mid- to upper-end hotels generally offer a safe to protect smaller valuables, some of these simply are not large enough to accommodate the kind of full-sized laptop computers that business-class travelers bring with them for several days of work on the road. However, even when the hotel-room safe is large enough to hold larger equipment, the electronic locks on these safes may be easily cracked by even an amateur thief with just a little practice.[7] Moreover, hotel staff also often have a master key or code that can open any private room safe in the establishment.

Don't Let Your Devices out of Your Sight, Ever

In light of these significant areas of physical security vulnerability, the question for users today is how can you protect your devices while traveling? It may seem straightforward, but, while at the airport and on the plane, simply never let these devices out of your sight. Ever. At the restroom, kiosk, restaurant,

---

[7]Lifehacker, Adam Dachis, "Crack Almost Any Electronic Safe with the Bounce Technique," http://lifehacker.com/5853610/crack-almost-any-electronic-safe-with-just-a-bounce, November 14, 2012.

lounge, bar, shoeshine, etc., keep your hands on your equipment. It's also important to recognize that while checked baggage is out of sight, it's also out of your control. If you lose a bag of clothes and a favorite pair of shoes, that's one thing. If you lose your work laptop or tablet with all of your passwords and data, that's an entirely different thing. As bags go around a crowded baggage carousel, with people milling about all looking for their own bags (and not paying any attention to the people around them), this provides a perfect opportunity for a thief to snatch and grab an expensive-looking laptop case. In a blink the thief can be lost in the crowd with no recourse available to the victim. This threat is magnified significantly by the fact that a plane ticket isn't required to enter the baggage claim area, so the number of potential thieves casing a carousel is essentially unlimited. For these reasons, a fundamental tenet of communications technology physical security is to never put a laptop, tablet, mini, or phone in checked luggage. Most of us are likely to avoid putting these rather fragile items into our checked luggage, out of fear of breakage. But what about smaller, less delicate items that still hold our data? Have you ever put a USB flash drive or other portable, backup hard drive into checked luggage? A lot of people do.

Transitioning from public to secured areas is another point of vulnerability. It is always uncomfortable to take our shoes off and put them, along with our wallets, watches, and phones, into the big plastic security bins and watch them ride away on the conveyer belt while we put our feet on the marks and raise our arms for the 360 degree scan. (Tad much? Definitely an issue for a different forum.) While this dance on the civil liberties tightrope progresses, be sure to keep a careful eye on your devices (which you should put into the same bin) at the security checkpoint. Don't step through into the scanner until you see your device(s) physically pass into the X-ray machine.

As an additional precaution, it might be worthwhile to consider adopting a nonstandard laptop carrying case. As Microsoft's web site advises: "The traditional black laptop bag can be an invitation to thieves, because they know exactly what's in there. It's a good idea to pick an unconventional-looking bag for your laptop. The less obvious it is that you're carrying a computer, the better."[8] Any kind of physical camouflage that you can adopt (e.g., generic bag, no organization identifiers on your machine) to diminish the probability that you will be targeted by a thief looking to steal expensive consumer electronics lowers the chances that your computer and data will end up in the hands of a thief. Keeping your proverbial head down in these circumstances can avoid unwanted attention.

---

[8]Windows, "Protecting Your Laptop when on the Go," http://windows.microsoft.com/en-us/windows7/protecting-your-laptop-when-on-the-go.

Thieves aren't looking for victims just in the airport or at the hotel. Because they're also looking for targets to take advantage of on the plane itself, an in-transit physical security imperative is to never place your laptop or tablet in the overhead bins. Sometimes, the bin you put your things in is several seats away; sometimes it's behind your seat or with no clear line of sight available. Not only is it easy for a thief to steal valuable electronics from the overhead bins, particularly if you take a nap on the plane as so many of us do, it also is likely that your equipment will be damaged by the weight of another person's bag, by an impact during turbulence, or by falling from the bin as someone else carelessly pulls their own luggage out.

Don't Let Strangers Touch Your Devices

Here, we're drilling into the issue for emphasis, but don't allow strangers at the airport to use your laptop. Common sense? Maybe so, but we're all susceptible to the tricks and cons that thieves will use to get their hands on our equipment. Not you? What if someone's missed her connection and she's just got to send a quick e-mail to her spouse because she lost her phone? Well dressed, polite, sad eyes…? What if his service is down and couldn't he please just send a quick e-mail to let his daughter know he'll be late? Don't you want to help a grandmother keep her grandchildren from worrying about her? Of course you do, and thieves know that you do, and will take advantage of your good nature in any way that works. Also be very aware if someone is trying to look over your shoulder or otherwise look at your screen or keyboard. Just wanted to see what the scores were—sorry. Just wanted to see the headline—sorry. No one has any business looking at your screen or keyboard for any reason. If someone is impolite enough to do it, even if just trying to catch a score, shut it down and move away. It is better to be a bit on the prickly side socially than to let your login credentials or password fall into the hands of a thief.

If you do need to leave your laptop behind in the hotel room when you head out for work, it may be a good strategy to leave the "Do Not Disturb" sign on the door, in an effort to prevent hotel staff from entering.[9] There is, of course, no guarantee that this will keep hotel personnel from entering and stealing valuables you've left behind, but it may contribute to the impression that your room is a less-attractive target than a room that staff are authorized to enter.

As with any valuables you'd like to keep secure, it is critical to not leave your laptop or tablet unattended in a conference room or convention hall. Relatively isolated, commercial, public spaces in unfamiliar places with transient

---

[9]Lifehacker, Alan Henry, "How Can I Make Sure My Laptop Is Secure While I Travel with It?" http://lifehacker.com/how-can-i-make-sure-my-laptop-is-secure-while-i-travel-1495527128, January 6, 2014.

occupants invite the attention of opportunistic thieves looking to steal valuable electronics used for presentations, meetings, demonstrations, etc.

What if It Gets Stolen?

If your machine is stolen or lost, Apple's "Find My iPhone/iPad" service (discussed in Chapter 7) has a similar (and free) analog for Apple computers called "Find My iMac." This product can be used to help track down a lost or stolen Mac. For Windows machines, third-party software products such as Prey (preyproject.com) and LoJack (lojack.absolute.com) offer very similar functionality to that available through Apple. As the names imply, this software tends to be more useful in the recovery of a laptop after accidental loss (left in the back of a cab or in a Starbucks) than as a tool to combat purposeful theft. A sophisticated thief can, for example, instantly erase a stolen device, rendering these tracking methods ineffective for purposes of retrieval.

The critical issue here is how can users protect their data when they're on the road? As discussed in Chapter 6, first and foremost it is essential to encrypt your hard drive and other devices per your company's data retention policies. Encryption should always be used in conjunction with a strong password policy—don't write your password on a sticky note on the laptop itself! Where theft is involved, a strong encryption and password scheme can limit the potential damage a user incurs to the actual cost of the device itself. When a user's data are protected through strong encryption, the computer, tablet, or phone becomes no more than a paperweight for a thief. As discussed in Chapter 5, always be extremely careful when using any unsecured wireless network while on the road. Don't use an open wireless network or hotel wired network for transmitting or receiving sensitive information that could be of value to a thief, and always use a corporate VPN whenever possible.

Additional Reading

For more on how to keep your data safe on your physical devices, see the following links and visit our web site at www.10donts.com/physical:

- *PCWorld*, "Keep Your Laptop Safe and Secure While You Travel", an article focusing mainly on pleasure/vacation travel: www.pcworld.com/article/2062781/keep-your-laptop-safe-and-secure-while-you-travel.html.

- Massachusetts Institute of Technology (MIT) Information Systems and Technology, "How Do I Protect My Laptop While Traveling?", guidelines focused on academic employees traveling with institutional devices: http://kb.mit.edu/confluence/pages/viewpage.action?pageId=4262903.

- Lifehacker, "How Can I Make Sure My Laptop Is Secure When I Travel with It?", a set of casual, consumer-focused guidelines, including both hardware and software recommendations: http://lifehacker.com/how-can-i-make-sure-my-laptop-is-secure-while-i-travel-1495527128.

- Lifehacker, "How I Got My Stolen Laptop Back Within 24 Hours Using Prey", a specific recounting of a laptop recovery procedure using the Prey software and service: http://lifehacker.com/5838440/how-i-got-my-stolen-laptop-back-within-24-hours-using-prey.

- Microsoft, "Protecting Your Laptop when on the Go", the Redmond software giant's recommendations for device preparations before travel and steps to take while traveling: http://windows.microsoft.com/en-us/windows7/protecting-your-laptop-when-on-the-go.

- BBC Travel, "Six Ways to Shield Your Laptop", a set of advisories on preventing laptop damage while traveling, as well as loss or theft: www.bbc.com/travel/blog/20121213-six-ways-to-shield-your-laptop.

- *USA Today*, "How to Use a Laptop when Traveling", an article which focuses on protecting a laptop when traveling to remote and less-trafficked areas of the world: http://traveltips.usatoday.com/use-laptop-traveling-11234.html.

Conclusion

Where Do We Go from Here?

Our professional intersection with—and investment in—the material we try to condense and describe in this book goes much deeper than our somewhat removed role as authors. We do hope that here we've been able to offer an easily digestible, essentially linear (entertaining?) framework for both understanding and, even more important, contending with emergent and constantly evolving threats to end users' data security. Broad consumption of even some of the cautions we offer, by sophisticated non-techies trying to function in an environment where the rules of play—and even the game itself—are constantly in flux, has potential to stem some of the truly mind-boggling data and security losses we've all read about and unfortunately even experienced first-hand.

We have a deep professional interest in the emerging questions concerning end user data security. There will always be work…. But like everyone else we are experiencing this "information age" explosion of possibility and vulnerability as spectators in what likely will be viewed by historians as the greatest single moment of evolution in our collective identity as a species. The Borg… perhaps not. But the emergence of virtual community that we're seeing today is simply 21st-century in its proportions—with all that comes along with that period designation. The good and the bad are unfolding simultaneously as we experience what it means to navigate in the virtual world.

As a broad, macro-level societal pattern, what we're seeing not surprisingly is that the vast majority of people just want to be a part of, and enjoy the benefits of, the connectivity that we have come to rely on in so many ways. Open the gates; open the gates! But within this mix, inevitably—with us since the serpent and the apple—is the need for caution and suspicion. There is just no way around the fact that with all of our virtual interactions on the Internet today there is an ever-present danger that requires a thoughtful approach and measured, careful handling.

Intelligent, sophisticated users can contend with these dangers. It starts with watching out for your data—be suspicious. As a basic point of departure, use common sense. Check your credit card and bank statements regularly for any irregularities. Some people do this as a matter of course; others don't. But unless you're regularly checking, small or seemingly inconsequential variations can easily go unnoticed, leading to bigger problems down the line. Report any abuses of your accounts or any suspicious or unauthorized charges that show up. These could be a signal that your accounts have been compromised by digital thieves who've accessed your personal data. Engage the system. Allow the entities you put your financial trust in to intercede at the institutional level on your behalf.

But, you're not on the boat alone. Today, more than ever, these large financial institutions are alert to their own vulnerabilities to virtual attack and exploitation. Size is apparently not a road block to modern virtual thieves, who may be even more likely to see larger banks as an attractive target. For example, on August 28, 2014, Charlie Osborne, writing for *Zero Day*, reported that the FBI was investigating a Russian hack of at least five American banks, including JPMorgan Chase.[1] The banks will, we hope, inform any of their customers made vulnerable through this latest security breach, and perhaps offer them formal guidelines or suggestions for remediating any damage to their personal accounts or online identity. It is critical that private end users affected by these attacks follow the official communications sent by their bank to limit the scope of the damage.

Don't Make It Easy for the Bad Guys

Sometimes, it's up to you to determine whether something is wrong. If you experience any strange behavior or functional slowdowns on your home wireless network, it's time to reboot the system, change your password, or call for help. For most readers, none of these steps is going to be entirely second nature. These maintenance activities are just not part of most people's everyday routine-even sophisticated users—and so likely carry with them some element of uncertainty or trepidation. You are not alone. It can sometimes feel like it in the middle of the night when your Internet stops working or your mobile devices fritz, but there are lines of support you can tap into. The IT staff at your office, online Help resources, even work colleagues who've gone through similar kinds of experiences can help you with these basic maintenance steps.

---

[1]ZD Net, Charlie Osborne, "FBI Investigates Hack of JPMorgan, Other US Banks," www.zdnet.com/fbi-investigates-hack-of-jpmorgan-other-us-banks-7000033080/, August 28, 2014.

Don't make it easy for criminals to get access to your data. As we highlight at the beginning of the book, any kinds of clues or hints as to what your password might be are just what thieves are looking for. Don't write down your passwords in an obvious location—this just invites security failure and loss of control over your property. Another convention worth adopting to help improve the security of your devices on the margins is to avoid spelling your passwords out loud as you enter them! Obvious? Not necessarily, particularly if you have a complex password that requires some concentration to enter. In this digital world, the importance of maintaining physical security just cannot be over emphasized. You never know who might be listening when you're sounding out "*IspentmyvacationinSt.Louis*"!

Toward this end, it is good practice, sane practice, to change your passwords often. Consistent with one of the major themes running through the book, the more often you can change your password, the less vulnerable your data are likely to be, but doing so comes at the price of convenience, as you take the time to actually do it. Yin and yang, pro and con, security and convenience—there is always a balancing act that has to be in focus as the virtual threats we face evolve and become more difficult to address in static ways. Similarly, it is important to use different passwords for different services and also for different devices.

Be Suspicious, and Trust Your Instincts

We all live in the real world, with real risks—but also with real time constraint trade-offs and mental load trade-offs. There are only so many passwords that you can keep straight conveniently, and there are only so many that you can keep up with if you're constantly changing them. This approach has got to become second nature so it consumes less energy and represents a more manageable cognitive load. Once it becomes habit, and some kind of predictable cadence emerges, it becomes easier to adopt a more stringent approach to password security.

With this resource issue in focus, it may be useful to think in terms of levels of security. You might maintain a few "high-level," very strong passwords for your most critical services, but you don't necessarily need to retain this kind of stringent gate for less critical accounts. You can probably get away with using "lower level," less-stringent passwords for what might be thought about as "throwaway" accounts or less important services. This might include a shopping account for a random Internet merchant that you plan to use only once, for example. It just isn't as critical that you protect this kind of transient connection with a complex key, because if it is compromised nothing of value to you is likely to be lost.

The threats to the security of your data are emerging more and more through various online channels. As we discussed in depth in Chapter 1, it is increasingly important to always verify the authenticity of an e-mail, text message, or web site before providing your password or any other personal data that could be stolen, sold, or used by a pirate looking to get rich. Keep a close watch on all of your devices. Be wary when something feels out of sync or a program or application seems to be functioning differently than it has in the past.[2]

Be cognizant that there really are bad actors out there looking for targets. Things like fake antivirus messages suddenly popping up and asking for money to fix a nonexistent problem should always feel sketchy. Strange software on your computer that you don't recognize, new toolbars in your browser that you didn't mean to install, anything that feels at all out of the ordinary to you should never be taken for granted or ignored. Don't assume that you're just imagining things or misremembering what you installed on your machine.

We are creatures of habit. We pay attention to patterns—our brains function by connecting the dots—and as a consequence we tend to notice when something in our immediate environment changes, feels different or off, or just doesn't smell right. Don't disregard your instincts. Trust them. Here, it is much better to be too suspicious than too forgiving. The potential personal, financial, social, and professional consequences for any kind of nonchalance are just too high. Let hyper-alert become the new normal.

The likelihood is that if it feels like something is wrong, then there is probably something wrong. Don't just close annoying pop ups, which are only going to return again and again. Either investigate the source of the problem yourself, or get someone to help you do so. Or if you can't, then report what's going on directly to the IT department (at work) or qualified repair professional (for personally owned devices) at a convenient big box store like Best Buy or H.H. Gregg. The Geek Squad is there to help you figure out some of the security issues you may not have the experience to handle yourself.

Keep the Home Front Safe

These aren't just work-related threats. Although your home may be your castle, it is not a fortress. People you don't know that well come in and out of it, and you're not always watching them closely while they're there. If someone has been in your home (e.g., baby-sitter, landlord, contract professional) and your computer or other devices seem to be acting differently, check them out. Don't convince yourself you're imagining things when you may not be.

---

[2]Techworld, Roger A. Grimes, "11 Sure Signs You've Been Hacked," http://news.techworld.com/security/3500234/11-sure-signs-youve-been-hacked, February 3, 2014.

Although it can be psychologically difficult to frame security issues in this way, sometimes it is important to take proactive steps to protect yourself and your valuable personal data against intrusions from someone whom you've trusted—but maybe shouldn't have.

The virtual and the physical dimensions of the security questions we examine are beginning to overlap in strange and unpredictable ways. In our discussion of physical security threats, we reflected on the emergence of apps that can allow criminals to get the key to your home printed at a hardware store by simply taking a picture of it. In August 2014, two researchers took this approach somewhat further. They demonstrated proof-of-concept through which they were able to create a "bump" key (a type of master or skeleton key) merely by obtaining a photo of the keyhole![3] These universal bump keys can potentially be printed by even a poorly funded, small-time thief at home, thanks to the prevalence and falling cost of "3-D printers," which facilitate the production of physical objects from digital blueprints.

We truly are living in a brave new world where technology is in many ways surpassing our current understanding of conventionally recognized boundaries associated with identity, property, security, and community. When someone can walk up to our front doors, take a picture of the lock, and half an hour later let himself in with a key he printed in the basement, what is clear is that rules of engagement have changed in fundamental—even unrecognizable—ways.

We have tried to stay away from conventional analogies to physical homes and neighborhoods in our treatment of the security issues and the virtual setting that defines the boundaries of the questions we address. However, when these worlds intersect in such an unconventional, and so 21st-century, way, it is hard to avoid drawing attention to the convergence of the old and the new worlds in which we're living and trying to operate safely, effectively, and productively.

Don't leave your machines (or your front doors!) unprotected. Take advantage of new data protection services offered by your employer, your telecom provider, or your e-mail or cloud storage company. If your employer offers antivirus, encryption, or other security software for use on personally owned devices, make use of these measures. They are often provided to employees free of charge and can ultimately save users a lot of time, money, effort, and other resources otherwise spent on retrieving data, dealing with identity theft and outright financial losses, and generally trying to get themselves back to par after a loss.

---

[3]*Wired*, Andy Greenberg, " These 3-D Printed Skeleton Keys Can Pick High-Security Locks in Seconds," www.wired.com/2014/08/3d-printed-bump-keys/?mbid=social_fb, August 26, 2014.

Watch for New Technologies

Become a more informed consumer as it relates to the digital devices you use and the virtual services you consume. Watch for announcements from telecoms and cloud or e-mail providers about new services that they're offering. Often, they're optional when they first come out. But take advantage of the opt-in as soon as it becomes available so you can preempt the vulnerabilities these new services are designed to address.

For example, Yahoo! will offer end-to-end encryption to their e-mail users by 2015.[4] This service will provide a significantly heightened level of security because data in transit are no longer "visible" to criminals in readable form. If you're a Yahoo! Mail user, opt in when you have the choice, because the sooner your data are protected, the fewer opportunities thieves will have to get their hands on your e-mail.

Another example is the cloud storage provider Dropbox, which made some changes to its service offerings in late summer of 2014. Most of the media attention these developments drew focused on Dropbox's lowering of its per-gigabyte price to compete with Microsoft and Google. However, Dropbox also made some important security enhancements to its Dropbox Pro service. These included the ability for end users to share files and folders with someone on a time-limited basis, setting access to expire after a certain point. Dropbox also added the ability to remotely wipe files from a lost or stolen device.[5]

Some of these more muscular services, while enhancing security, inevitably require you to think again in terms both of security and convenience. For example, as we discuss early on, Google currently offers an optional two-factor authentication for its Gmail service. Although this may seem like a hassle—particularly if you check your e-mail as frequently during the day (and night!) as most users with smartphones typically do—consider opting in and adopting two-factor authentication, particularly if Gmail is your primary e-mail provider. It could save you unnecessary heartache and pain.

The advances in security you can take advantage of today aren't limited to software and cloud services. Watch for other new features from hardware manufacturers, telecoms, or third parties that can also allow you to better protect your devices and data: new biometrics, new password managers, new ways to

---

[4] *PCWorld*, Ian Paul, "Yahoo Mail to Support End-to-End PGP Encryption by 2015," www.pcworld.com/article/2462852/yahoo-mail-to-support-end-to-end-pgp-encryption-by-2015.html, August 8, 2014.

[5] Ars Technica, Jon Brodkin, "Dropbox Matches Google and Microsoft Pricing for a Terabyte," http://arstechnica.com/information-technology/2014/08/dropbox-matches-google-and-microsoft-pricing-for-a-terabyte/, August 27, 2014.

track your lost or stolen devices. For example, in August 2014, researchers at the Georgia Institute of Technology demonstrated prototype software on the Android operating system that can encrypt any and all communications to and from a device, regardless of the particular app used.[6]

This represents an entirely new phase of in-transit data security for end users that isn't even on the market yet, but don't let too much time pass when it becomes available before adopting. One of the inevitable realities of the virtual landscape we all must navigate today is that as soon as a new level of security is developed, criminals immediately begin the process of unraveling its secrets and chipping away at the protections it offers. Certainly, particularly in light of the tremendous rate of change we've seen in programming sophistication, the benefits of even the newest protective screens can be assumed to be relatively short-lived at best. No matter the size of the swatter, a bigger, badder bug is always just around the corner.

Keep Your Hands off Old Machines

Given the increasingly serious threat posed by virtual crime, although we are creatures of habit, we can no longer afford to be sentimental when it comes to the devices and programs we use to store and manipulate our data. We like our ratty T-shirts and it's hard to get rid of old things, but this shouldn't apply to computing devices, no matter how battered and familiar, which it is absolutely critical to regularly keep updated. Discontinue use of all "dinosaurs" or other obsolete devices, as these simply carry with them too many liabilities to be of any kind of consistent viability. It's not just hardware that becomes obsolete. You must also keep all of your devices up-to-date with software patches from operating system manufacturers and application manufacturers.

It can be annoying to restart your computer and integrate these patches, particularly if you procrastinate and wait until you have 15 to 20 minutes worth of updating to do, but, it is essential that you don't allow any of your machines to get behind, even by a few weeks. The nature of the threats to which they're exposed today is constantly evolving, so continuing to regularly take small steps forward is the best approach currently available.

If your employer seems to be stuck in the proverbial "stone age" when it comes to hardware and software upgrades (which some of the tragic tales we've related here, such as T.J. Maxx, among others, illustrate in an all-too-immediate way), speak up. Say something to someone in a position to do something. Forward current articles about the dangers of out-of-date devices

---

[6]*Wired,* Andy Greenberg, "This Android Shield Could Encrypt Apps So Invisibly You Forget It's There," www.wired.com/2014/08/m-aegis-android-encryption/?mbid=social_fb, August 19, 2014.

and software to your supervisor, or even your supervisor's supervisor...carefully! Smart money would even go as far as to leave a copy or two of *10 Don'ts* behind in the executive conference room, with pages strategically flagged! There are a lot of misconceptions about what modern computing hardware/software looks like, particularly among employers who are loath to spend money on new devices and upgrades when "We just bought you all new computers/phones three years ago!" But today, with the rate of change that we're seeing across all spectrums of the virtual computing landscape, three years is positively Jurassic.

Dangerous, outdated devices aren't just relics lying around your own office or garage; sometimes you get stuck somewhere without your devices—lost in transit, left behind, dropped, stolen, etc. If you are forced, temporarily, to use an antiquated device or operating system, never transmit any of your sensitive data on it. Wait. It is always better to avoid this kind of exposure whenever it's possible to do so. It's not that a thief is necessarily lurking or that malware is poised to infect at the moment you log on to a machine with an unsupported operating system. But, a thief could be doing precisely that. The probability that you get snared or infected or identified increases every time that you take chances with old equipment or outdated software.

Maintain Your Privacy

One of the biggest issues that technology users face today is the loss of privacy and anonymity as it relates to online activities. Do some research on your own. Find and use a secure or non-traceable browser, as discussed in Chapter 6, to help keep your online activities as private as possible. Get some help from an IT professional if you aren't entirely fluent in the process of adopting new software. There is, of course, no perfect solution to the problem of snoops interested in your business. If they really want to look over your shoulder—if they're committed to doing so—the options start to get pretty scarce. But, you can make it more difficult for snoops to initiate or sustain unwanted intrusions into your personal business. We deserve to be able to operate autonomously online. Sometimes, we have to fight for that privacy and sometimes we need help to achieve it.

Most Important—Be an Educated and Informed Digital Consumer!

Another theme we've returned to throughout the book is that the exposures we have to contend with are emergent. They are like viruses, mutating and evolving in response to the prophylactic interventions security professionals devise. In light of this dynamic landscape, it is crucial to remain current. Be on the lookout for new threats. Read computer magazines, web sites, or blogs. *Wired, MacRumors, CNet, PC Magazine*, and others of the genre are all aimed toward nontechnical to moderately technical users. These resources can help you to keep aware of current hacks or Advanced Persistent Threats that are making the rounds on the Internet. Staying current is increasingly important as the cycle of offense and defense becomes more and more abbreviated.

Remember, this isn't necessarily a process that you have to engage in on your own. Your company's or organization's IT department may circulate warnings or advisories of recently discovered attacks, and what you need to do to steer clear of the threat they represent. Although it can feel like this doesn't pertain to you, because there are a lot of potential targets out there, and it is very seductive to think that "It won't happen to me…," don't ignore these cautions. Read them. If they call for a particular action (e.g., change your password) or non-action (e.g., don't open an attachment from XXX.com), the likelihood is that if you follow these instructions your machine won't be exposed to a threat that could otherwise lead to the loss of your data or other broad vulnerability with costly systemic consequences.

We're also in the game. Keep an eye on 10donts.com and our Facebook and Twitter pages for up-to-date information on current security threats as well. The bottom line here is that because the nature of the threats to the security of your data will continue to mutate and evolve, you can't become complacent and assume that because you were safe yesterday, you're safe today. This is something that needs to be on your mind.

Although the game is changing, some of the old, proven cons and snares are still out there. Ransomware, drive-by downloads, social engineering tricks, etc.—criminals will continue to use many of these same old scams as long as they continue to work. Variants of phishing scams, attacks on cloud providers, and wireless networking attacks will continue to emerge. Governmental agencies and for-profit firms focused on your money will continue to find new ways to "snoop" on private users. Variants totally unrelated to those threats we currently know about, employing methods we can't predict, will be developed and spread and be addressed and continue to evolve in response.

An old adage is relevant here: follow the money. That is exactly what criminals on the Internet will continue to do. As long as there is money, there will be criminals focused on getting their hands on it. These threats will never disappear. They will most certainly continue to mutate, and while there may be intermittent, temporary reprieves from some of the most virulent, these threats are a definitional companion of the virtual infrastructure in which we and all of our collective data are now embedded. These threats will never disappear.

Where there are valuable resources, crime is an inevitable consequence, which is a predictable, regrettable aspect of human nature. Yet, there also are probabilistic realities that bear on the calculus used to weigh risk versus return.

Criminals will always look for targets that carry with them the lowest probability of getting caught in the end, with the easiest escape routes, the most concealed entrances, or other security weaknesses. Twenty-first-century digital thieves are no different from the bank robbers of the 20th century—they will look for the easiest targets and attack those first. Don't make yourself one of the easy targets.

A Christopher McDougall quote is relevant here, albeit with a slightly different indication. As McDougall famously wrote in *Born to Run: A Hidden Tribe, Superathletes, and the Greatest Race the World Has Never Seen*:

> *Every morning in Africa, a gazelle wakes up, it knows it must outrun the fastest lion or it will be killed. Every morning in Africa, a lion wakes up. It knows it must run faster than the slowest gazelle, or it will starve. It doesn't matter whether you're the lion or a gazelle—when the sun comes up, you'd better be running.*

Here, it may not be necessary to outrun the fastest lion; it may be enough simply to not be the slowest gazelle. As the Internet more and more becomes a vehicle for digital commerce, what is clear is that it will become even more inextricably connected to dollars—massive dollars. Digital data are big money, on a truly epic scale, and getting bigger all the time. As some of the recent corporate data-security breaches have highlighted—T.J. Maxx and Target among others—these numbers are big enough to attract the most sophisticated criminals. Don't make it easier than it needs to be for the bad guys, the government, or corporations to get their hands on your data. Always try to keep at least some of the other gazelles in your rear-view mirror.

Index

A

Advanced Persistent Threat (APT), 38, 108

Anti-malware programs, 5

B

BitLocker, 73

Bluetooth hacking, 88

Boundless Informant surveillance
program, 59–60

Bring your own device (BYOD)
COPE, 79
employee's device, 78
IT department, 77
operating procedure, 21st century, 78
physicall secure, phone
ActiveSync makes options, 84
Find My Phone, 83
password isn't enough, 82
startup PIN, password/fingerprint
key, 81–82
right things by reporting, 80

C

Cloud services
accessibility, 32
Adobe's Creative Cloud, 26
cloud-based storage, 33
data breaches, 29
data storage, 30
description, 25
Dropbox, 26
informal relationship, 28
Instagram, 28

quasi-technical term, 27
reliability, 32

Cross-site scripting (CSS), 5

CryptoLocker malware, 114–116

D

Data at rest, 65, 73

Data in transit, 65

Data privacy. See Snooping

Data protection. See Snooping

Dinosaurs
caution, 105
desktops and laptops
fragmentation, 101
Google App Store, 101–102
iOS users upgrade, 103–104
iPhone, 103
security watch, 103
mechanics of, 105
operating system, 100
parents' computer, 93
software
expiration date, 94
Mobile Apps, 95
new software, 95
Windows, 99
Windows 95 operating system, 94
Windows XP (see Windows XP)
system and software
configurations, 104
Windows reboot, 105

Dishfire surveillance program, 62

DuckDuckGo (DDG) search engine, 73

Get the eBook for only $10!

> Now you can take the weightless companion with you anywhere, anytime. Your purchase of this book entitles you to 3 electronic versions for only $10.

This Apress title will prove so indispensible that you'll want to carry it with you everywhere, which is why we are offering the eBook in 3 formats for only $10 if you have already purchased the print book.

Convenient and fully searchable, the PDF version enables you to easily find and copy code—or perform examples by quickly toggling between instructions and   applications. The MOBI format is ideal for your Kindle, while the ePUB can be utilized on a variety of mobile devices.

Go to www.apress.com/promo/tendollars to purchase your companion eBook.

Other Apress Business Titles You Will Find Useful

How to Speak Tech
Trivedi
978-1-4302-6610-5

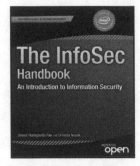

The InfoSec Handbook
Rao/Nayak
978-1-4302-6382-1

Advanced API Security
Siriwardena
978-1-4302-6818-5

**Platform Embedded
Security Technology
Revealed**
Ruan
978-1-4302-6571-9

**Healthcare Information
Privacy and Security**
Robichau
978-1-4302-6676-1

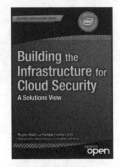

**Building the
Infrastructure for Cloud
Security**
Yeluri/Castro-Leon
978-1-4302-6145-2

**Expert Oracle
Application Express
Security**
Spendolini
978-1-4302-4731-9

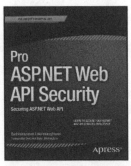

**Pro ASP.NET Web
API Security**
Lakshmiraghavan
978-1-4302-5782-0

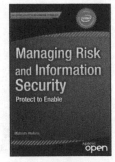

**Managing Risk and
Information Security**
Harkins
978-1-4302-5113-2

Available at www.apress.com